FONDREN LIBRARY

Southern Methodist University

DALLAS, TEXAS 75275

WITHDRAWN
SMU LIBRARIES

WITHDRAWN
SMU LIBRARIES

EDWARD S. CORWIN
AND THE
AMERICAN CONSTITUTION

Edwin S. Corwin. Printed with permission from the American Philosophical Society.

EDWARD S. CORWIN AND THE AMERICAN CONSTITUTION
A Bibliographical Analysis

KENNETH D. CREWS

Foreword by Alpheus Thomas Mason

Bibliographies and Indexes in Law and Political Science, Number 2

Greenwood Press
Westport, Connecticut • London, England

Library of Congress Cataloging in Publication Data

Crews, Kenneth D.
    Edward S. Corwin and the American Constitution.

    (Bibliographies and indexes in law and political
science, ISSN 0742-6909   ; no. 2)
    Includes indexes.
    1. United States—Constitutional law—Bibliography.
2. United States—Constitutional history—Bibliography.
3. Corwin, Edward Samuel, 1878-1963—Bibliography.
4. Corwin, Edward Samuel, 1878-1963. 5. Political
scientists—United States—Biography. I. Title.
II. Series.
KF4546.A1C74   1985   016.34273'029 [B] 84-19185
ISBN 0-313-24233-X   (lib. bdg.)   016.   34730229

Copyright © 1985 by Kenneth D. Crews

All rights reserved. No portion of this book may be
reproduced, by any process or technique, without the
express written consent of the publisher.

Library of Congress Catalog Card Number: 84-19185
ISBN: 0-313-24233-X
ISSN: 0742-6909

First published in 1985

Greenwood Press
A division of Congressional Information Service, Inc.
88 Post Road West, Westport, Connecticut 06881

Printed in the United States of America

10   9   8   7   6   5   4   3   2   1

368706

To
R. W. C.
B. J. C.
and
E. S. C.

Contents

Foreword

ALPHEUS THOMAS MASON

*McCormick Professor
of Jurisprudence, Emeritus
Princeton University*

I first met Edward Corwin when I came to Princeton University as a graduate student in 1920. Until his death in 1963, Corwin was always my friend and mentor. I knew his strengths and weaknesses, and he remains in my mind the greatest constitutional commentator of all time. Nevertheless, the outstanding puzzle about Corwin is that, although his many articles and monographs constitute a major work, he never produced what could be fairly rated a major work in terms of scope. He never wrote the comprehensive constitutional study he proposed. That is why studies such as this book by Kenneth Crews are so important. My guess is that no one knew the man, scholar, and teacher better than I--until this book became available.

Corwin was a scholar and teacher by example rather than precept. He published voluminously and discussed subjects of current interest. He once told me that he never spent more than eight weeks on anything he wrote-- hard to believe. But Corwin's talents were generally incredible. I doubt whether he spent more than half an hour on an undergraduate lecture. His practice was to scribble a few notes on a discarded envelope and from them to speak brilliantly. His teaching will always continue, however, from the lessons of his life and from the abundance of his publications, all revealed in this book.

Preface

"If judges make law, so do commentators."
Edward S. Corwin, 1923

Edward S. Corwin's constitutional theories have influenced scholars and lawyers throughout the twentieth century. Arthur M. Schlesinger, Jr. and Henry Steele Commager acknowledge their debt to Corwin's analysis of presidential powers. Louis W. Koenig recently highlighted the modern relevance of Corwin's observations about presidential powers and about federalism and the relationship between the national and state governments.[1] Professor Corwin remains a subject of modern interest for the continuing vitality of his ideas and for his historic prominence in politics and constitutional law. A biography and bibliography are the fountainhead for understanding Professor Corwin. Much has been written about his theories, so this book turns attention to Corwin the man. His writings and scholarship are invariably major elements of the biography, and its central thesis relates Corwin's personality to his flood of publications. But I do not detail the content of his writings. Instead, I attempt to reveal Edward Corwin's influences and experiences in youth, his development as a professor, and his ventures with politics. The bibliography offers ample references to other essays elaborating on Corwin's many theories.

Knowing a scholar's life enhances the understanding of his theories. Many historians and political scientists have been active in politics and have served in government. Such experiences can influence the scholar's studies. Corwin's personal politics affected his theories and writings. His Republican background and support for Theodore Roosevelt clashed with Woodrow Wilson's conservative views and probably generated Corwin's criticism of the League of Nations. In the 1930s, Corwin served the Franklin Roosevelt administration, and his scholarly writing in turn vigorously endorsed the New

Deal. Edward Corwin's personal disappointments with Roosevelt, however, compelled the Professor to reevaluate virtually all of his political theories. Corwin enjoyed the independence of academics, but he also confronted the influences of current events and of his personal involvement in them. The study of Corwin proves that constitutional theory is fluid. Just as Supreme Court interpretations change through the years, constitutional scholarship can vary with individuals, circumstances, and events. The American Constitution is more than secure principles; it is a living reflection of the people who study it, live by it, and look to it for guidance.

My interest in Corwin began with Schlesinger's frequent reliance on him in The Imperial Presidency. I was then an undergraduate at Northwestern University, and the next year Corwin was the topic of my senior thesis for the History Department. Under the direction of Professors Jamil S. Zainaldin--now with the American Historical Association--and Jack C. Thompson, I studied Corwin's changing theories during Franklin Roosevelt's administration. The Court-packing debacle came to light, as did the Professor's growing criticism of the president during World War Two. My research during that academic year of 1976-1977 also demonstrated the need for a new Corwin bibliography. I owe tremendous credit to previous bibliographies, but those works were far from complete, included bothersome inaccuracies, and lacked annotations.[2] I attempted to complete the Corwin bibliography as part of my senior thesis.

From Northwestern I proceeded to law school at Washington University and to law practice in Los Angeles. I persevered with the project all the while. My legal education allowed better insights into constitutional law and opened new research techniques. In the summer of 1983 I paid my first visit to Princeton University where my wife and I shared an intense week with Edward Corwin's personal papers. The private correspondence and reams of newspaper clippings evinced fresh views of Corwin's life, from his early years in Michigan through his last years at Princeton. The papers also included a vast collection of Corwin writings published in newspapers and periodicals available in few libraries and not indexed anywhere. Local newspapers and popular magazines carried some of Corwin's most important letters and articles. Those contributions to American political thought might have been virtually inaccessible had Corwin himself not collected them and had Princeton University not preserved them.[3] Although the bibliography lists every known publication by Edward Corwin, it may never be absolutely complete. Other essays, reviews, and letters to editors may continue to surface with future research. I would be eager to learn of all discoveries. On the other hand, I never intended the bibliography about Corwin to be complete. The number of books and articles mentioning the Professor is nearly endless, and I have not attempted to compile the thousands of reviews of Corwin's books.

The long process of studying Corwin has required the assistance of many friends, scholars, and libraries. I give special thanks to critics who read all or part of my manuscript drafts and who lent needed comments and encouragement: Dr. John Allen Gable of the Theodore Roosevelt Association, Professor John V. Richardson, Jr. of the UCLA Graduate School of Library and Information Science, and Professor Emeritus Alpheus Thomas Mason, Corwin's successor as Princeton's McCormick Professor of Jurisprudence. John Gable has been a close friend from the time I discovered Corwin and has been enthusiastic guidance and inspiration. John Richardson instructed me on successful publication processes and will soon become my professor as I enroll in his school's doctoral program. Professor Mason first met Corwin in 1920 and worked with him as a student, colleague, and friend for the next forty years. Professor Mason's personal knowledge of Corwin made his comments about my manuscript and his foreword to this book deeply meaningful and reassuring.

Princeton University and its staff deserve warm gratitude for making my project possible. Nancy Bressler of the Mudd Manuscript Library and Earle E. Coleman of the University Archives assisted efficiently and tirelessly during my research at Princeton and during my long series of correspondence for advice and information beginning in 1976. Laura C. Ford, the University Counsel, and Thomas H. Wright, the University Secretary, quickly granted permission to quote from Edward Corwin's unpublished correspondence and other materials protected by copyright. My thanks extend to others who granted similar permission. Frances Dwight Buell gave consent to quote from her unpublished essay on Corwin and from correspondence by Raymond Leslie Buell, her late husband and a former Corwin student. The Corwin Papers include two letters from Vice President Richard Nixon, and the former president graciously allowed me to quote from them. Mary Rossiter allowed me to quote from a letter by Clinton Rossiter, her late husband and another Corwin protege. The American Philosophical Society provided the frontispiece photograph.

A bibliography is a tribute to libraries, and I have benefited from libraries and librarians across the country. I must acknowledge particularly the collections I visited and used extensively: University of California at Los Angeles, Chicago Public Library, Library of Congress, Los Angeles County Law Library, Los Angeles Public Library, University of Minnesota, University of Missouri, New York Public Library, University of North Carolina, Northwestern University, Princeton University, University of Southern California, and Washington University. Numerous other libraries in every part of the country responded to my requests for details about articles in local publications. I must also thank friends who understood and supported my project. Janet F. Katz of Washington, D.C. scrutinized microfilm at the Library of Congress to find an elusive Corwin letter to a New York newspaper. Edmund Morris, biographer of Theodore Roosevelt, provided correspondence between Corwin and TR. Finally, all of my thanks, gratitude, and appreciation inadequately describe my debt to the persons to whom I dedicate this book: my parents, Ralph Wilson Crews and Betty Jo Crews, who supported me throughout my undergraduate and law school years when this study began; and my wife, Elizabeth St. Clair Crews, who appreciated the time and energy that a book requires and who worked by my side at Princeton to make the research more efficient, pleasant, and successful. Friends call my work on this book a labor of love, but my family's support is the best demonstration of that devotion.

Los Angeles, California
July 9, 1984

Part One
Life of Edward S. Corwin

1
Presidents and Preceptors
1878-1920

Edward Corwin was a public educator. As a professor at Princeton University for virtually his entire career, Corwin became one of the school's most popular and respected teachers. But his talents went far beyond the classroom. His prolific writings embraced the full scope of constitutional law and history, and the Professor was a demanded public speaker. He thus shared his insights and wit with readers and listeners around the world. He quickly became known as the "law professor" at a university without a law school, and he emerged as one of the leading constitutional and political commentators of the twentieth century. Concentration and dedication characterized Professor Corwin.

Many professors nurture side interests. A Shakespeare scholar writes movie reviews; a mathematician indulges in poetry. But Corwin seemed to have given not only his professional career, but also his entire life, to the Constitution. Late in life he wrote to the Princeton town paper--in one of his numerous letters to editors-- objecting to truck traffic in front of his house. The letter was at last a touch of Corwin dealing with common noise problems. But he finished with a constitutional argument for regulating traffic. He even cited a Supreme Court decision.[1]

Corwin's unswerving interest in law generated his high academic reputation and standing. Through extraordinary concentration and dedication, he was able to write twenty books, edit several others, and compose over 150 articles and as many book reviews. He made the "letter to the editor" a favorite pastime, and the news media frequently sought his opinions. But Corwin's concentration was not narrowness. Constitutional law touches nearly all aspects of the government, and Corwin wrote about most of them--from international relations to income taxes and from Supreme Court justices to presidential disability. These dedicated talents belonged to a man of diverse background.

Edward Samuel Corwin was born on January 19, 1878 on a farm near Plymouth, Michigan. Farms were undoubtedly a significant part of that community lying some twenty miles west of Detroit and fifteen miles due east of Ann Arbor. Farming was part of Corwin's early life, although he later listed his father, Frank Adelbert Corwin, as "Township Treasurer."2 The Corwin ancestors came to America from England long before the American Revolution. Matthias Corwin came from Warwickshire, England and reputedly helped found three American towns: Ipswich, Massachusetts in 1634; New Haven, Connecticut in 1638; and Southold, New York in 1640. Corwin's great-great-great-grandfather, Stephen Corwin, was a quartermaster under George Washington at Valley Forge. His son, Stephen, was one of four guards to witness the hanging in 1780 of Major John Andre, a co-conspirator of Benedict Arnold. Corwin's great-grandfather, Isaac, fought in the War of 1812.3

This lineage could have made Edward Corwin think that more than Plymouth, Michigan awaited him. But Corwin remained in Michigan for many years, attending local grade schools and Plymouth High School. His early avocation was science, particularly astronomy. A grandfather primed his interests with books on astronomy and with outspoken opposition to the theory of evolution. A great-uncle kept weather instruments and advised farmers on when to sow and reap. Corwin's mother offered a touch of politics. Dora Lyndon Corwin was a suffragette and teetotaler at a time when alcoholic consumption was as much a political concern as it was a matter of morals, health, or religion.4

Politics, law, and history soon became young Edward's passion after entering the University of Michigan in 1896. As a freshman, he studied European history under Professor Frank H. Dixon, who years later joined Corwin at Princeton. But Corwin often said that his keen interest in constitutional law arose from late-night discussions and debates with law students sharing his Ann Arbor boarding house. These conversations must have evinced not only Corwin's hidden interests, but also his knack for arguing controversial topics.5

He continued to study European politics and history in his sophomore and junior years, as well as economics, Latin, rhetoric, French, philosophy, and mathematics. Constitutional studies rapidly dominated his curriculum. Corwin took Professor Andrew C. McLaughlin's course, "Political and Constitutional History of the United States," as a sophomore, and McLaughlin immediately became Corwin's mentor for the rest of his student life at Michigan. The University of Michigan had a

strong program in constitutional studies, led earlier
by Professor Thomas McIntyre Cooley, the eminent scholar
and former judge of the Michigan Supreme Court. Corwin
recalled seeing Cooley once. It was Cooley's last public
appearance before his death in 1898. He was only in
his 70s, but Corwin sentimentally called him "a pathetic
sight." "I nearly wept," he recalled.6
     McLaughlin, known affectionately as "Andy Mac," had
come to the University of Michigan in 1891. He was the
History Department's rising star. McLaughlin's early
writings centered on the history of the Old Northwest,
but he later wrote extensively on constitutional history. Corwin's senior year was almost exclusively under
McLaughlin's tutelage. He studied "Constitutional Law
and Political Institutions of the United States" and
took two research courses from the mentor. While
reviewing the Dred Scott Case of 1857, the Supreme Court
puzzled Corwin by concluding that part of the Missouri
Compromise violated the Due Process Clause of the Constitution. The Court had not previously construed the
clause as a substantive limitation. McLaughlin was
stumped. He could not understand its meaning, either.
"If he doesn't know, nobody does," thought Corwin, and
he began a lifetime exploration of due process.7
     Professor McLaughlin returned Corwin's admiration
in kind. McLaughlin moved to the University of Chicago
in 1906, and there he shared with graduate students the
experience of reading Corwin's final examinations. "I
cannot teach this young man anything," thought McLaughlin
at the time, "he already knows all about the subject."
Corwin won solid acclaim at the University. He was
elected president of the class of 1900 and graduated
Phi Beta Kappa.8

     With Ph.B. degree in hand, Corwin took a short break
from university life to teach high school history
courses. His first position was at Ishpeming, Michigan
in the western part of the state's "upper peninsula"--a
long way from Plymouth and Ann Arbor and deep in the
hills and forests south of Lake Superior. The next year
he went to The Polytechnic Institute in Brooklyn, New
York. In a lengthy letter from the Brooklyn principal,
Corwin learned that his "work at the School will be that
of directing the development of the Department of History, with the other duties that must be assigned in any
well-ordered school." Reading further, Corwin discovered
that the "other duties" stemmed from his "experience
as a principal." His responsibilities would include:
"watching over boys as they pass to and fro about the
building, occasional (sometimes regular) supervision
of assembly-rooms when the grade-officers are called
away from their rooms, the care of boys on recess, and
other duties that must be classified as police-routine."

As for class instruction, the principal assured Corwin that regimented controls of the past had given way to a "sense of hearty freedom and initiative in each teacher and pupil." It seemed little wonder that Corwin stayed in Brooklyn only one year, particularly in light of his later adversion to administrative tasks at Princeton.9

Corwin returned to the University of Michigan and Professor McLaughlin in 1902. For two years he continued his study of American history, serving all the while as Andy Mac's teaching assistant. For the third academic year, 1904-1905, Corwin accepted a fellowship at the University of Pennsylvania and moved to Philadelphia. Professor John Bach McMaster advised him that year in the completion of a doctoral dissertation, and that school awarded Corwin a Ph.D. in spring of 1905. Although Corwin's passion was clearly constitutional history, his dissertation examined the alliance between France and the United States during the American Revolution. Later published by Princeton University Press, Corwin's study boldly reinterpreted the critical alliance. Rather than focus on the drive for harmony between the two nations, Corwin found that France's motivation for ties to America stemmed from its rivalry with Great Britain for sea and colonial power. He was twenty-seven years old and already a talented historian.10

With his student career ending, Corwin attended a leisurely dinner at the McMaster home. He pondered with the Professor about his plans and pending unemployment. McMaster told his good student about a new venture at Princeton University called the "preceptor program." Woodrow Wilson had been president of Princeton only three years, but he was rapidly modernizing the school's curriculum. The word of "preceptorships" spread quickly among scholars throughout the country. With Princeton a short ride from Philadelphia, and with Corwin's demonstrated excellence, McMaster gave his student a confident recommendation: "Why don't you run over to Princeton and apply to Woodrow Wilson for one of those preceptorships they're handing out over there?" The advice was well received.11

Clutching McMaster's "extraordinarily flowery" letter of introduction, the young Edward Corwin made his first expedition to Princeton and his first bid for a university career. He arrived in the central New Jersey town on a Monday morning in June 1905 and made his way to Prospect House by eleven o'clock. Prospect was the University president's official residence and the place where Corwin knew he would find Wilson. Built in 1849, the house stood majestically at the western head of Prospect Street, near the center of campus. A servant met this stranger at the door and advised him that President Wilson was with another caller; Corwin would have to wait. The wait must have seemed interminable. The eager recruit undoubtedly considered his uncertain future as he nervously paused in the home of the nation's most famous university president. Woodrow Wilson was moving the old "College of New Jersey" out of its quiet days and into the light of a modern "Princeton University." Wilson sought fifty new preceptors for the challenge. Corwin wanted to join the ranks. It was a unique opportunity exclusively for prize scholars.[12]

The wait was only ten minutes, but it was long enough to build drama for Corwin. He recalled that entering Wilson's study "was one of the most memorable moments of my life. Mr. Wilson seemed to me easily the most impressive human being I had ever met." Wilson described the preceptor program, and Corwin spelled out his qualifications. After their brief meeting, Corwin followed the president's directions and walked across campus to Mercer Street to meet Professor Winthrop More Daniels, Chairman of the Department of History, Politics, and Economics. The combined department had been formed in 1903, and the rubric "Politics" was Wilson's preference for the field; he found it more accurate than "Political Science." The Daniels meeting was another pleasant and constructive interview, and the conversation even included Corwin's salary needs--a topic scrupulously avoided in initial interviews unless employment appears certain. Indeed, Corwin received word from Wilson just two or three days later that he was on the staff at Princeton. Wilson also offered the salary Corwin viewed necessary "if I was ever to induce my creditors to lose interest in me." The first year's salary was $1600.[13]

Edward S. Corwin was standing on his own in the world of higher education. He had been described as "short and stocky in figure," but that aphorism belied his image. He carried a rigid stature and personality. His light complexion, fine features, and piercing eyes held attention, and he adorned himself with neatly cropped hair--parted high on the left--and pince-nez glasses, all in true Woodrow Wilson style. His manner of speaking was most idiosyncratic. Whether in casual conversation or classroom lectures, Corwin spoke hurriedly and with a sharp, clipped accent. He sometimes left students behind and sometimes simply befuddled. An apocryphal story involves one of his students who could not decipher the "dishulroo" concept mentioned regularly in Corwin's lectures. A knowing graduate student settled the dilemma: it was Corwin's peculiar slurring of "judicial review," a critical topic in constitutional law.[14]

Moving to Princeton in the summer of 1905, Corwin resided for the next four years at the campus Bachelor Club, where his colleagues soon called him "the General." The moniker stuck for life. Names were a problem for Corwin. Through an irrepressible alliteration with "Corwin," he was plagued by "Edwin." Correspondence came

to "Mr. Edwin S. Corwin;" articles were published by
"Edwin S. Corwin;" and newspapers interviewed "Professor
Edwin Corwin." He battled this mistake, but seldom won.
In a letter to Senator H. Alexander Smith in 1945, Corwin
added a firm postscript: "Please tell your Secretary
my first name is Edward, not Edwin."15

To his friends and close colleagues, however, this
new Princetonian was "Ned." Affectionate and admiring
letters addressed to "Dear Ned" came throughout his
life. Names held an undeniable importance. Corwin
eschewed "Edwin;" Wilson preferred "Politics;" and the
entire school only recently adopted the name "Princeton
University." It was symbolic of the institution's transformation now led by Wilson. Academic standards were
falling; students crowded classes in record numbers.
Lectures dominated teaching techniques, increasingly
separating students from professors. Preceptor were
to curb those trends by being a "guide, philosopher,
and friend" to the students. Wilson enlisted forty-five
new preceptors in 1905 at the rank of assistant profes-
sor.16

Princeton established a four-year program for its
undergraduates, with the preceptors taking roles in the
junior and senior years. Each course had a uniform three-
hour format. Two hours each week were for lectures by
professors. The third hour was for "conferences" with
preceptors. Corwin, and each of the other preceptors
in the history field, had eleven seniors and fourteen
juniors under his guidance. The conferences brought
students and preceptors together on familiar terms and
for concentrated education; usually only three to five
students met at a time. Corwin lamented the unwieldy
volume of reading required for the conferences. He soon
divided the conferences to meet twice each week for
thirty minutes, thereby distributing the reading load.
Reading assignments covered jurisprudence classics:
Wilson's The State, Holland's The Elements of Jurisprudence, Maine's Ancient Law, Jenks's Law and Politics
in the Middle Ages, Hall's A Treatise on International
Law, Ostrogorski's Democracy and the Organization of
Political Parties, and Markby's Elements of Law. "At
least I got an education," remarked Corwin. If the tomes
burdened him, one could only sympathize with the stu-
dents.17

Corwin had his own ideas about teaching, leading to
his first conflict with Wilson. Even before classes
began in September 1905, Corwin decided that final examinations were incompatible with preceptor teaching.
He temeritously raised the issue at a meeting of preceptors led by Wilson himself. Wilson disagreed with the
young man, and examinations continued. Corwin persevered
in other manners. In a 1906 article in the Michigan
Alumnus, Corwin noted the flexibility of some departments

to give preceptors limited control over examinations, including determining their relative importance and whether students would even take them. He complimented Wilson's "openness of mind. . . ." By 1908 Wilson had left all of these issues to the individual departments.18

The preceptor program was a success, as was Corwin himself. The program changed the college atmosphere from social life to engrossing studiousness. Corwin observed the symptoms: town establishments were quiet in evenings, and casual discussions among students changed from sports to intellectual concerns. Like the preceptor program, Corwin was also a success at the university. Princeton promptly renewed his one-year contract for four more years at $2000 annually. Soon well-known as "the General" and willing to speak out when he disagreed with Wilson, Corwin captured the respect of fellow Princetonians. The mutual respect between Corwin and Wilson from their first meeting also grew through ensuing years. Disagreements did not tarnish that respect. Rather, respect allowed disagreements in a gentlemanly fashion. The two men agreed, however, on one of Wilson's most controversial propositions.19

Wilson was increasingly concerned about the growing importance of "eating clubs" on campus. The clubs were like non-residential fraternities; students lived elsewhere, but clubs provided meals and social events for members. Clubs conflicted with the intellectualism Wilson nurtured at Princeton. He therefore proposed a "quad plan" in 1907 to replace clubs with residential colleges. The trustees immediately supported Wilson, but virtually all support buckled when alumni and faculty criticism jeopardized contributions and financing for the project. The "quad plan" was Wilson's first critical defeat, and he nearly resigned. But Corwin was on Wilson's side, as were most preceptors. Personal loyalty to Woodrow Wilson, rather than actual merits, dictated Corwin's position.20 As the two academicians agreed and disagreed on university policy, they had mixed political opinions. Corwin was "born a Republican" in Michigan--a state which in the late nineteenth century was customarily endorsing Republican candidates. Wilson was a Democrat. Wilson nevertheless admired the Republican Theodore Roosevelt, who became president in 1901. That admiration wore thin through the next several years, particularly as Wilson pondered his own political future.21

Wilson's goals were hardly secret, and Corwin and others proffered advice. Corwin generally favored Roosevelt's liberalism. Roosevelt was expanding the presidency and federal government in foreign affairs, business regulations, social welfare, and military concerns. Never again, thought Corwin, would the nation accept a conservative Democrat like Grover Cleveland. Wilson was that kind of conservative. Those conservative and liberal beliefs finally clashed at an informal department meeting in late spring of 1908. Gathering on a Friday evening at the home of Professor Paul van Dyke, the faculty discussed a resolution supporting the Roosevelt administration. When Wilson spoke, "he raked TR's record fore and aft, emphasizing especially the laxity of TR's constitutional principles and his efforts to break through all controls, including the lines between state and national power and the lines between the departments." Corwin bristled. He supported Roosevelt's policies, and he knew that Wilson's platform would scarcely bring him political triumphs. Corwin answered Wilson's challenges. Wilson even showed some pleasure through Corwin's rebuttal. Indeed, the overwhelming vote for Roosevelt at that evening's meeting apparently did not faze him. When Wilson described the occasion years later, he spoke of how "a young man named Corwin got up and wiped the floor with me." Corwin thereafter took credit for persuading Woodrow Wilson toward liberalism.22

Corwin must have impressed Wilson; in December of that year Wilson gave the preceptor a tremendous vote of confidence. Wilson's little volume on American history, <u>Division and Reunion</u>, had drifted badly out of date since its original publication in 1893. University challenges and political thoughts absorbed Wilson, so he needed a new contributor to handle the writing. In December 1908 he tapped Corwin for the job. Corwin had few publications by that time. He was thirty years old, had edited one book on Scandinavian history, had written one scholarly article, and had a few book reviews to his credit. Wilson clearly did not select Corwin for his record; he chose him out of confidence. Corwin was also not the object of favoritism; Wilson's political ambitions could not afford the controversies an inept co-author might arouse.23

<u>Division and Reunion</u> was all it promised to Corwin. It was Wilson's expression of confidence, Corwin's opportunity for a professional reputation, and--as he gratefully acknowledged--a good source of income. The timing was also perfect. The book offer came in December 1908, and Edward Corwin was engaged to marry Mildred Sutcliffe Smith the following June. The manuscript pushed that perfect schedule. After two delays of nuptials, Corwin and Mildred Smith were married on June 28, 1909. They immediately embarked on eight weeks of honeymoon in Italy. The travels depleted their savings, but income from the book awaited them. The newlyweds were suddenly allowed "comparative affluence."24

Mildred Smith was from Ypsilanti, another town in the Plymouth-Ann Arbor corner of Michigan. She was a slender woman with strong facial features, and she maintained herself in conservative formal attire--as did her husband and most Princeton personnel. Mildred would apparently never have a strong outward role in Edward's professional life, although in dedicating a book to her, the Professor called his wife, "My most encouraging and constructive critic." But Mildred was a reliable companion. The couple traveled extensively and hosted numerous social evenings at home.25

Corwin began a period of critical development in 1909. Aside from personal changes effected by marriage, his professional ventures blossomed. From 1909 to 1911 he published a sequence of articles in the <u>Michigan Law Review</u> and in the <u>Harvard Law Review</u> on constitutional law and history. He examined due process, judicial review, the Fourteenth Amendment, and the Dred Scott Case. He was finally tackling questions that stumped Professor McLaughlin so long ago, and top law reviews accepted his studies. Success also brought opportunity. The University of Michigan invited Corwin to join its faculty. Corwin called Wilson with the news; Wilson promptly promised Corwin a permanent professorship and wrote to Professor Daniels: "I hope you will exert all the influence you can upon him to retain him." That year, Corwin obtained a five-year appointment with Princeton at $2800 annually. He became the highest-paid preceptor. Corwin was promoted in 1911 to full professor. He was thus a permanent faculty member. He was also becoming a leader in the Snuff Club, an informal gathering of faculty members. Snuff Club members shared their intellectual and social interests and often shaped academic policies through their combined influence with John Grier Hibben, Wilson's successor in the president's office.26

Woodrow Wilson's career also changed during those years. He left Princeton in 1910 after losing a showdown over graduate school issues and was elected governor of New Jersey. Wilson was instantly on his way to the presidency. Corwin's association with Wilson--as a colleague, co-author, and antagonist on academic and political issues--generated attention as Wilson became nationally famous. The Professor, though Republican, stayed close to Wilson. Personal loyalty allowed his support for Wilson on the "quad plan" issue, and it might have worked again. But Corwin had something to gain this time: the excitement of presidential politics and the prestige of a White House association.27

Baltimore hosted the 1912 Democratic Convention where Wilson gained the nomination. Corwin wrote Governor Wilson to request a convention floor pass. Wilson complied, and Corwin packed himself to Baltimore. There William G. McAdoo--a campaign manager and successful New York attorney--was Corwin's friendly escort to the convention. Corwin's visit fell on June 27, and that

evening he watched William Jennings Bryan deliver his
spectacular oratory for a resolution opposing candidates
representing or under obligation to J. Pierpont Morgan
or "any other member of the privilege-hunting and favor-
seeking class." Bryan further demanded expulsion of
such delegates. The convention turned to riot. Corwin
watched as delegates and politicians fired their anger
and shook their fists. The shouting drowned Bryan's
voice. After a series of tense confrontations on the
platform, the resolution passed by a lopsided vote--
without the expulsion clause.28

Edward Corwin voted for Woodrow Wilson, and Wilson
became president of the United States on March 4, 1913.
Corwin immediately tendered counsel. California's treatment of Japanese residents strained Sino-American relations, and Corwin insisted in a letter to his friend
in the White House that claims of "state's rights" did
not protect California's actions. The problem was for
the federal government to resolve through its treaty
powers. Wilson balked. The president responded: "I
do not feel by any means as confident as you do as to
the power of the Federal Government in the matter of
overriding the constitutional powers of the states
through the instrumentality of treaties. . . ." Wilson
had put aside Corwin's opinions before.29

The issue of federal treaty powers was more than a
passing thought for Corwin. That same year, Henry Holt
and Company published his first book, National Supremacy:
Treaty Power vs. State Power. Corwin argued in his
concise text that the powers constitutionally allocated
to the states do not restrict the federal government's
potential treaty powers. The United States could enter
a treaty, for example, with Japan regarding the treatment
of its citizens in America. The treaty would pre-empt
California's control of the issue. Professor Corwin
sent a copy of the book to Wilson to emphasize his
point. Just to be sure, he also sent a copy to Theodore
Roosevelt, adding in a letter: "You will find the position I have taken to be in accord with the tenets of
the Progressive Party." Roosevelt was leaving to explore
the Amazon River but responded that he wanted to meet
Corwin after returning in spring of 1914.30

Corwin's political commitment to Wilson was weak from
the beginning. His argument in 1908 on behalf of
Theodore Roosevelt was sincere--not just a debate with
Wilson. But Corwin's dedication to the impressive
Mr. Wilson was a personal draw and a commitment to the
man who gave him a career at Princeton. With Wilson
in the White House, and Corwin staying at Princeton,
the personal relationship began to fade. The great
enthusiasm for Wilson in the 1912 election was gone by
1916. In a letter to the New York Evening Post shortly

before the 1916 election, Corwin attacked Wilson's handling of foreign policy and stated his strong support for
Charles Evans Hughes, the Republican candidate.31

With or without Corwin's support, President Wilson
was back for another term. Within a month of his second
inauguration, Wilson asked Congress to declare war on
Germany. Back at Princeton, Corwin became a political
and philosophical supporter of the commander-in-chief.
Even before Wilson's appeal, the Professor had written
in the Daily Princetonian about "the Pacifism which
springs from lack of hearty belief in the future of our
institutions, a scepticism which strikes hands with personal disinclination for the hardships of war. It is
this sort of Pacifism which constitutes a new national
problem." He was writing for student readers who could
be either distressed or stirred by his words, but "the
General" nevertheless concluded: "And war, on its dangerous side, enlists first our young men. The chivalry
of youth so dictates, and so does natural equity. It
is their heritage that demands protection--they stand
at the threshold of the generation which is threatened."32

Corwin was shooting patriotic guns. He soon called
for conscription and obligatory military training. Even
before the 1916 election he urged the government to build
its military preparedness before establishing a lasting
foreign policy.33 Corwin might have been behind the
war campaign, but his statements were not truly Wilson-
ian. He did not rally people around their leader or
mention one way or the other what Wilson preferred.
Corwin simply expressed his own views about the nation
and the world--not Wilson's views, not anyone else's
views. Corwin was sincerely the objective professor
free of constraints. But there were influences. His
call to arms by the youth of America and his rhetoric
about dangers and hardships of war were easily remini-
scent of Theodore Roosevelt, Corwin's early political
hero.

A professor cannot stay objective at all times,
especially one making a call to arms. Corwin went to
Washington in fall of 1917 to lend his services to the
Committee on Public Information, the government's sophis-
ticated public relations agency. Together with Professors Frederic L. Paxson of Wisconsin and Samuel B. Harding of Indiana, Corwin edited a compendium of details
about the war called War Cyclopedia. The book was an
extended glossary of every imaginable term, name, and
concept related in any manner to the Great War. His
service in Washington was brief, but back at Princeton
he was appointed First Lieutenant in the R.O.T.C. "The
General" could now wear a uniform and be saluted. He
was Lieutenant Corwin, but always the professor; his

primary duty was teaching in the Summer Military Course from June to August of 1918. He was proudly serving his country in the national emergency.34

The war's end and the ensuing League of Nations fight allowed Corwin to resume his objective professor role. He also showed unequivocally that President Wilson had not captured his endorsement. Wilson went to Paris in 1919 and brought back for Senate ratification the Treaty of Versailles and the Covenant of the League of Nations. Senate opinion was deeply divided, and opponents led by Henry Cabot Lodge proposed reservations to the covenant, restricting America's obligations in international disputes. Wilson held firm. The League was his plan for an ordered, peaceful globe; Lodge's concerns could not be allowed to destroy it. Professor Corwin was caught between two old friends. One of the Professor's early works was editing a volume on Scandinavian history for the History of Nations series. Lodge was the editor-in-chief of the entire series, and it was still in print with new editions in the making. Wilson, of course, was Corwin's colleague. Corwin took sides with Lodge.35

Edward Corwin's writings clearly supported ratification of the covenant, but only with Lodge's reservations. Unlike Lodge, however, he demonstrated some compromise, particularly on freedom of the seas. Wilson's early peace plan called for absolute freedom of navigation, which the League would enforce. Corwin took a British perspective. He wanted to allow Britain its superior navy to protect other traffic and to preserve world peace. Soon, however, he wrote in favor of world control of the seas, with substantial control by Britain and other countries, but only if that control followed a constitution.36 Corwin's writings were scholarly. His public appearances, however, were sometimes fervid. Speaking before the Hoboken Forum Association in that northern New Jersey town, the Professor reportedly "ripped the covenant to shreds." Declaring that any nation in the League would lose its sovereignty and freedom of choice, Corwin insisted that the United States must remain aloof from European concerns. He hardly sounded like a supporter at all--with or without reservations.37

The Senate never ratified the covenant, and the United States never joined the League of Nations. In the 1920s, Corwin joined advocates of American adherence to the World Court, one element of the League plan. But that hope never materialized, either. The Wilson years thus yielded mixed results for the Professor. He was everywhere known and introduced as a Wilson colleague. The connection gave him prestige and credibility for his writing and speaking. The connection also provided his first major writing project when he prepared the new edition of Division and Reunion. All differences with Wilson aside, Corwin prepared yet another edition in

1921. But one must wonder whether Corwin was completely comfortable with his Wilson ties. He never had the chance to join the administration, and his informal advice was rejected. He and Wilson also differed on numerous matters from final examination policies to the League of Nations. Yet Corwin was inescapably tied to Wilson, and on the whole the connection was a firm endorsement and a source of popular appeal.

2
The General
1920-1932

The Wilson years brought enormous expansion of Corwin's scholarly achievements. His writings carried an outstanding and independent quality. Corwin no longer relied on Wilson for academic stature, although the presidential association must have brought welcome attention. A 1914 article surveying the Professor's career commented that he had only one book to his credit, but he was already familiar as "one of the most conspicuously keen of contemporary students of the Constitution." Professor Corwin held his colleagues' attention with novel theories about judicial review, due process, and federal treaty-making powers. That year he spoke at the Lake Mohonk Conference on International Arbitration on the subject of treaty powers. He held a firm liberal position. Meeting with academic, business, and political leaders at a resort near Poughkeepsie, New York, Corwin demonstrated the federal government's constitutional authority to make treaties regulating activities ordinarily reserved for states. He called for expanded federal powers in social and economic policy through treaties. Only then could the United States keep abreast of world economic policy.[1]

Corwin was advocating a reposturing of traditional constitutional powers. Shifting powers from states to the federal government was constitutional, according to the Professor, even though the move altered authority over local activity. These breaks from traditional constitutional order made Corwin a liberal by contemporary standards. His most telling early essay on constitutional order appeared in 1920. Corwin traced popular veneration of the Constitution from its origins down through the twentieth century. He found the worship fading during the Civil War, when President Lincoln put the Constitution aside in favor of practical action to meet current demands. The end of veneration was not maudlin news for Edward Corwin. He endorsed the trend. He wanted the Constitution to meet modern needs and to be flexible for the nation's unanticipated challenges.2

Edward Corwin's liberalism revealed itself not only in his constitutional theories, but also in the publications carrying his essays. The New Republic, Nation, and the Review (later the Weekly Review) carried Corwin articles regularly for several years after 1915. He used these liberal exponents to call for national railroad legislation, child labor reform, and a better League of Nations plan. Liberalism even entered his scholarly articles in otherwise-staid law reviews. In the Harvard Law Review he argued that state control of police powers must give way to federal powers, and in the Michigan Law Review Corwin again imitated Theodore Roosevelt's policies by supporting resource conservation efforts.3

Like Corwin's feelings about Wilson, his liberalism had significant exceptions. The most salient deviation was his vehement opposition to the League of Nations without Lodge's reservations. Corwin even glorified the merits of isolationism. In spite of these views, however, Corwin genuinely favored the resolution of world disputes by some international body. He singled out the World Court for endorsement. Another touch of non-liberalism was Corwin's personal politics. In a 1920 letter to the New York Times, he continued attacks on the League and complimented Warren Harding--the Republican nominee for president. A short-lived conservative magazine, Harvey's Weekly, reported one of Corwin's critical comments on the League amidst the magazine's ludicrous jabs at James Cox, the Democratic Party's choice for president that year. While calling the nominee "Coxey" and denouncing his "Coxidized campaign," Harvey's Weekly applauded Corwin for explaining the League's real meaning. Again, the Wilson connection lent attraction and credibility.4

The Wilson ties were ironically deepening, even while Corwin distanced himself from the president's politics. In 1918 Corwin succeeded to Wilson's former position as the McCormick Professor of Jurisprudence at Princeton University. Now he was no longer just a colleague of the president and his hand-picked preceptor and co-author, he was following Wilson's academic growth. Corwin was forty years old; his accomplishments as a historian, political commentator, and educator received the highest honor Princeton's Politics Department could give. Corwin was the third holder of the McCormick chair. Named for Cyrus Hall McCormick of the International Harvester Company in Chicago, Wilson became the chair's first beneficiary in 1898. Professor William Franklin Willoughby maintained the position from 1912 to 1914.5

The writings mentioned above are a small sample from the extraordinary prolific period that Corwin began to enjoy in the late 1910s. The volume and diversity of his writings presented undeniable justification for his accolades and honors. Division and Reunion seemed to unleash Corwin's muse for research and writing in nearly all areas of constitutional law and history. Most of his articles and books in the 1920s were academic essays, and most of them saw print in law reviews and political science journals. He wrote commentaries on contemporary Supreme Court decisions, essays in favor of social legislation, and analyses of the balance of federal powers. The roles of the Supreme Court, Congress, and the president were beginning to intrigue the Professor. He had previously written on each of these branches, but in the early 1920s he began viewing them as interactive and cooperative branches. Wilson and the war demonstrated that powers could shift from Congress to the president, and the growth of social regulation moved powers from states to the federal government.

Regardless of his particular topic, Corwin focused on the relationship between law and society. This theme manifested itself most often in Corwin's growing belief that the Constitution should meet modern needs. Thus, if society demanded that the federal government remedy child labor problems, constitutional definitions of reserved state powers should not hinder progress. This philosophy was consistent with his early advice to Woodrow Wilson about Japanese settlers in California. If the state inadequately handled the matter, and the federal government had an interest, Washington should take action. With his sensitivity to society's perception of the law, Corwin brought his writings out of the exclusive world of scholars and lawyers. His most important attempt at popular writing began with The Constitution and What It Means Today, first published in 1920. That book dismantled the Constitution clause-by-clause and explained its meaning. The Professor was becoming a public educator; he was avoiding the jargon of legal studies and giving readers a concise understanding of the American Constitution, together with reviews of major Supreme Court cases.6

Corwin's essays and books brought enormous acclaim. Benjamin Cardozo, then a New York judge but soon to join the United States Supreme Court, observed in a personal letter to Corwin: "I find I have frequent occasion to draw upon your learning." Corwin's legal studies appeared in publications of wide circulation and put him in contact with people like Cardozo. Corwin also continued his history interests. He published a brief biography of John Marshall in 1919 and was thereafter known as a Marshall scholar. Marshall also gave Corwin a touchstone of constitutional philosophy. The early chief justice declared in one of his most celebrated rulings, handed down in 1819, that the Constitution must "endure for ages to come" and "be adapted to the various crises of human affairs." When Corwin invoked his call for a flexible Constitution to meet current needs, he called on the words of Chief Justice Marshall for support.7

The Professor embarked on another major historical work in the 1920s and 1930s. He began a biography of Edwin E. Stanton, the Secretary of War in Abraham Lincoln's cabinet. But apparently uncooperative Stanton descendants and expanding demands for Corwin's time compelled abandonment of the project. After futile efforts to pass the task to other scholars, Corwin finally made a single product of his work; he presented a paper in 1938 on "The Relations of Secretary Stanton and President Johnson" to the American Philosophical Society.8 History had a larger role in Corwin's scholarship than these few examples reveal. His comments on contemporary politics and legal developments offered a historical perspective. He understood presidential powers from their historical growth. He reflected on the judiciary's role by revealing its evolution through the years. History was Corwin's means of grasping the present and building for the future. He brought history to issues that seemed to have only immediate interest, and he demonstrated that lessons from the past could guide politics of the present.

Corwin's writings were scholarly, but his jurisprudence was populist. He believed that law and the Constitution should reflect human needs and expectations. Corwin was something of a populist in his professional style, too. More of his writings moved from narrow forums of law reviews and journals and into the familiar territory of newspapers and magazines. The New York Times printed Corwin's letters at a regular pace and quoted the Professor extensively on issues from Prohibition to the Scopes "Monkey Trial." Reporters discovered that Corwin had opinions on nearly every legal subject. One resourceful journalist interviewed Professor Corwin during a 1927 visit to Atlanta and discovered another touch of conservatism. Corwin demanded tough law-and-order on crime issues. He called for capital punishment and broader judicial powers. Corwin was generally conservative about the Bill of Rights. He carried strict views of free speech rights and, as he would later emphasize, of the separation of church and state.9

Corwin the liberal, conservative, populist, scholar, and commentator was still primarily a professor at Princeton University. Professor Corwin's courses sometimes included international law and administrative law, but the centerpiece of his curriculum was "Constitutional

Interpretation," an advanced course in the Politics Department. Politics became an independent department in 1924, emerging from the earlier combined Department of History, Politics, and Economics. As a teacher, Corwin was demanding and admired. "Con Interp," as his course was known at Princeton, was regularly rated the most difficult and still the best course available. With his rapid and staccato speaking, Professor Corwin fired his students with questions and more questions to illustrate theories of constitutional law. His physical command and intellectual awe confirmed the appellation "the General."[10]

Professor Corwin was the innovator of "Con Interp." He brought constitutional studies to liberal arts for the first time, without focusing solely on history. He taught constitutional law as a body of legal doctrines related to broader philosophical, political, and social concerns, and his style was that of a professor, rather than of a preceptor. Corwin argued in favor of lectures, despite student pleas for more informal discussions. Corwin also insisted that independent research enhanced teaching. Research was a source of inspiration. "Con Interp" in turn became an inspiration to students and a staple course at Princeton. His students included John D. Rockefeller III, Allen Dulles, Adlai Stevenson, and Syngman Rhee, as well as future scholars Raymond Leslie Buell, Alpheus Thomas Mason, and Clinton Rossiter. Corwin preferred teaching men, and Princeton was an all-male institution. He once admitted that he had liked teaching women when he was younger. He was probably referring to his short teaching assistantship at the University of Michigan from 1902 to 1904.[11]

Corwin was also the department's first chairman, holding the position from 1924 to 1936. He seemed to have had little desire for administration when he went to Brooklyn Polytechnic in 1901. The department head experience confirmed that suspicion, and Corwin delegated most duties to Professor William Seal Carpenter. But as a chairman he was still well-liked. Edward and Mildred Corwin opened their house on Prospect Street for frequent entertainment of colleagues. The nights with the Corwins brought cohesion to the department and offered informal occasions for spilling opinions and discussing university life. The Corwins never had children; their social life with students and faculty probably provided an extended family. The evenings also allowed Corwin to relax with wine for dinner and an occasional smoke afterward.[12]

Honors and opportunities came quickly by the late 1920s. For the academic year 1928-1929 Edward Corwin became one of the few prominent American professors to teach in China. Princeton had recently established the Princeton-Yenching Foundation in Peking to foster academic growth as that eastern country expanded its international influence. Dr. and Mrs. Corwin spent most of the year in Peking, teaching at Yenching University, Tsing Hua University, and Boxer Indemnity College. Corwin taught about constitutional and political systems, but he also traveled and learned much about the Chinese nation and peoples. He noted the political turmoil as China struggled for unification, and he dreaded the spreading poverty and famine. Yet Professor Corwin was optimistic about the country's future, particularly the future of Yenching University. He saw the school as a pocket of strength and spirit in a troubled land.[13]

The Chinese venture brought the Corwins tea with Madame Chiang Kai-shek and warm acclaim from their Peking hosts. The route to and from the Orient also took them to Hawaii, Japan, Korea, the Philippines, India, through the Suez Canal, to Italy and France, and finally to New York City. Reporters greeted the Professor back at Princeton and gathered his observations about the large and changing land he visited. As he reviewed the nation's challenges, Corwin proposed that China divide into two countries--North and South--to eliminate much internal dispute. After settling back at Princeton and the duties of teaching and writing, American law returned as the center of Corwin's attention. Corwin spoke once more on China, in early 1931, when he prophetically cautioned against the spread of communism.[14]

Speaking engagements came steadily, as did further honors. Professor Corwin became one of the few American members of l'Institut International de Droit Public in France. In 1931 he became president of the American Political Science Association.[15] He seemed to be atop the pinnacle of his career. He had come far from the days of leaning on the Woodrow Wilson association. Now his peers acknowledged Corwin as a foremost leader, scholar, and teacher. He was fifty-three years old in 1931, and he had accomplished most goals of professors. Students admired his teaching; Supreme Court justices read his commentaries; and colleagues made him leader of his academic department and professional organization. But Corwin's career was hardly at its climax. He had many years ahead, and the next several years would bring new opportunities, experiences, and ultimately radical changes for Edward Corwin. Those changes would advance his career, but not without substantial cost to the prominent professor.

3
The New Deal Revolution
1932-1937

Edward Corwin probably could have relaxed after 1932. He had completed his presidency of the American Political Science Association, and he was highly regarded as a historian, political commentator, and teacher. He also enjoyed his gardening, took in a little golf, and spent summers in Vermont. But 1932 was a fateful year for the Professor and for the nation. The Depression condemned the Hoover presidency, and Franklin Delano Roosevelt rode a landslide into the White House. The new president began his "100 days" of leading legislation through Congress to relieve the economic emergency. The government recast its purposes and powers with the National Industrial Recovery Act, the Agricultural Adjustment Act, and other legislation. The federal government was assuming authority customarily allotted to states, and Congress was delegating powers to the president and his agencies. It was a "revolution" endorsed by Congress and demanded by most voters to attack the Depression.[1]

These events touched Corwin's deepest interests. Roosevelt's New Deal raised issues of federal powers, judicial review, and constitutional flexibility--Corwin's forte. The New Deal's constitutionality was in question from its inception, and Corwin summarized it as a test of "the capacity of the Constitution to absorb a revolution."[2] His response to the New Deal was rooted in his writings and theories from two preceding decades, particularly regarding judicial review of legislation and presidential leadership of Congress. Judicial review is the power of courts to determine the constitutionality of legislation. Corwin acknowledged the authority of courts, but he frequently criticized the right of judges to create legal doctrine. In 1911, Corwin wrote that judicial review was established on "the doctrine of a fundamental law known only to the judges. . . ." He later added that judicial review "rests upon the assumption . . . that the judges alone really <u>know</u> the law," and he declared his long-standing principle: if the Constitution did not meet modern needs, the fault lay with its interpreters.[3]

The economic crisis required new interpretations of Congress's powers. Limited theories of the Commerce Clause and restricted delegation rights should not preclude modern demands. The courts must defer to Congress. In a speech at Princeton in November 1933, Corwin concluded that the New Deal signalled "the twilight of the Supreme Court" by ushering in legislative authority, rather than judicial authority, as the supreme rule of government. By adopting new powers, Washington was devising a "cooperative conception" of government. The New Deal was to Corwin a fusion of powers and a sense of cooperation between federal and state governments and among the branches of the federal government alone.[4]

The decline of judicial review was acceptable only with caution and only with strong presidential leadership. The president could make Congress aggressive and efficient. Corwin had long observed the need for presidential leadership. In 1919, he criticized President Wilson's lack of leadership in ratifying the Treaty of Versailles. Six years later he tied presidential leadership to popular legislation. He found that judicial review delayed "the effectuation of preponderant opinion in law" but would do so only until leadership assured that congressional enactments truly expressed firm, popular sentiment. The New Deal created the situation Professor Corwin envisaged: Roosevelt's leadership led to highly popular legislation, and judicial review could diminish.[5]

Some factors in Corwin's model were temporary; Roosevelt could not always be available for leadership, and the New Deal's need might end as the economy improved. Yet the changes wrought by Roosevelt were clearly going to be permanent. Corwin himself noted that a program like the NRA should survive the Depression, otherwise the emergency could recur.[6] Nevertheless, Corwin and others supported the radical changes invoked by the New Deal. The Supreme Court, however, had other ideas. It did not allow its review powers to wane. In 1935 the Court began striking down popular New Deal legislation as unconstitutional, despite a pro-New Deal signal it sent the previous year. In <u>Home Building & Loan Association v. Blaisdell</u> the justices upheld a Minnesota law relieving pressure on homeowners facing delinquent mortgage payments. Corwin cautioned that it was a weak signal. The state statute hardly represented the governmental overhaul demanded by the New Deal, and the law had a built-in expiration date.[7]

Corwin became known to the public and to the Roosevelt administration as a New Deal advocate. He was not a blind supporter; Corwin joined a group opposing Roosevelt's tax remission and credit system for funding state unemployment insurance. Corwin wanted a system controlled by the federal treasury. Still, Corwin has been criticized in retrospect for supporting the New Deal without carefully considering the alternatives, as he usually did in his scholarly work. Corwin was a welcome ally for the administration, which immediately enlisted his expertise. The Housing Division of the Federal Emergency Administration of Public Works hired the Professor in June 1935 for fifty dollars a day. The rate may have seemed low for one of the top constitutional scholars, but Corwin welcomed the opportunity to go to Washington.8

He had fulfilled most goals of a professor except for putting his theories to practice. Corwin's friendship with Woodrow Wilson did not bring a Washington appointment, and indeed Wilson rejected Corwin's advice on the government's treaty powers. The 1920s kept Corwin in Princeton with his writing, teaching, and other professional responsibilities. The 1930s and Franklin Roosevelt created new heights for Professor Corwin. He could assist with formulating policy, and a former student, John Dickinson, was an Assistant Attorney General overseeing much of that policy. For the administration, Corwin was a show of credibility. He was well-known as a foremost scholar, and his background as a Wilson protege and as an American Political Science Association president were attractive indicia of talent.

Government service also contributed to Corwin's scholarly growth. From his work in the Housing Division he authored a law review article on federal authority to provide low-income housing. When he told Benjamin Cardozo of his work, the justice asked Corwin not to send a copy of the essay--a relevant case was pending before the Court, and Corwin's work could be unduly influential. The government also wanted Corwin to do just what he did in his writings: be scholarly. When Assistant Attorney General Thurman Arnold sought Corwin's arguments in support of the Social Security Act, he specifically requested a historical analysis. Princetonian scholarship was blending successfully with Washington politics. Corwin was putting his ideas to work simply by providing the research and analysis he had always done. In turn, Washington had the Corwin imprimatur on the New Deal's liberal constitutionalism.9

The Carter Coal case brought Corwin's best opportunity to form policy. The Bituminous Coal Conservation Act regulated the wages and hours of employees at coal mines and taxed sales of coal from mines not complying with new regulations. The constitutional attacks reached the Supreme Court in 1936. The Court had already stricken other New Deal legislation, and Roosevelt was eager to try new defenses. With Corwin's help, Dickinson argued that Congress had the right to regulate matters such as prices and wages which were not part of interstate commerce itself, but only related to it. Congress had the power, he contended, to enforce its regulations with penalty taxes. The Supreme Court heard oral arguments on the case in March 1936, with Corwin sharing the lawyers' table. A crowd in the courtroom waited for the justices to grill the lawyers, leaving hints of their positions, but two days of oral arguments passed with hardly a remark or interruption. The Court had already struck down the National Industrial Recovery Act; it soon struck down the Coal Act, despite Corwin's good counsel.10

The Supreme Court's rulings against the New Deal stirred opposition not only from Corwin and the Roosevelt administration, but from much of the public as well. The New Deal was the central hope for recovery amidst a depression, and the Court was using narrow theories of interstate commerce and separation of powers to block legislation. The Supreme Court was suddenly the focus of desperate public attention. Politicians and commentators debated the dilemma and argued possible solutions-- or whether there were any solutions at all. The Supreme Court in 1936 comprised "nine old men" having an average age of 71 years. Roosevelt was completing a full term in office, and no justice had stepped down to allow a fresh appointment. Legislation passed Congress, but a judiciary from a different era nullified the effort.11

Corwin began writing profusely on the conflict. He wrote for newspapers and magazines and lectured on the radio to reach the general public with his analysis of the Court problem. Corwin's public notoriety was blossoming, and his name kept cropping up when talk turned to the Supreme Court. Soon he was mentioned--often mentioned--as a possible Court appointee. All he needed was a vacancy. Only one justice had to retire, and Corwin would be in line for the job. The Professor clearly had the prospect in mind. He joked with students about joining the Court, and reporters and friends approached him with the idea incessantly.12

Corwin had every reason to support the president's bid for re-election in fall of 1936. He could privately be grateful for the opportunity to advise the New Deal team in Washington, and he could contemplate joining the Supreme Court. Roosevelt could be sure of Corwin's allegiance to the New Deal, and the Court seemed a fitting culmination to a successful academic career. Publicly, however, Corwin endorsed Roosevelt's economic policies, such as his desire for a more even distribution

of wealth. In an interview for the Princeton University
student newspaper, Edward Corwin made two prophetic
observations. He underscored his support for the president by remarking that he would be in a second term and
thus not pre-occupied by thoughts of further elections.
And he mentioned obliquely some sympathy for Abraham
Lincoln who had to increase the membership of the Supreme
Court in 1863 to change its views. Corwin by no means
asked for expansion of the Court, but he tossed around
the subject with a sense of acceptance.13

The Professor as a political insider and public figure
had to learn caution with sensitive or controversial
topics. His learning came through some fairly paltry
examples. Corwin was one of sixty-six prominent intellectuals selected to receive honorary degrees on the
300th anniversary of Harvard University in the summer
of 1936. His speech for the occasion examined the dicho-
tomy between the Constitution itself and constitutional
law as developed by courts. For a little "comic relief,"
as he explained, Corwin referred in his speech to historical inaccuracies in the pictorial artwork on doors at
the new Supreme Court building in Washington. Corwin
had seen reports of the errors in the New York Times,
but he misguaged the topic's popular interest. For the
public, at least, his speech was lost in the controversy
of the Supreme Court doors. Washington newspapers dwelt
on the matter and checked every detail. Corwin finally
corresponded with the architect's office to resolve the
stirring questions. He conceded one error, held firm
on another, and expressed amazement about the whole
situation. The door issue, and an earlier complaint
about his using a quotation by Charles Evans Hughes out
of context, warmed Corwin for public controversy. These
incidents revealed that his statements were now in the
open domain for scrutiny, and that minor discrepancies
could detract from the larger point. People were more
interested in the Court's doors than in the critical
speech at Harvard; readers lost the meaning of Hughes's
statement by focusing on the context. These small controversies prepared Corwin for the weighty controversy
he shared with the Roosevelt administration the next
year.14

When Corwin wrote of the Supreme Court problem, he
generally recommended that the Court itself should provide the remedy. For example, the Court could simply
not hold itself bound to past decisions. It could therefore escape the New Deal rulings in the next case. The
president and Congress should also not feel bound and
thus free to keep passing progressive legislation. In
addition, Corwin recommended from time to time that
justices retire at age seventy. A regular turnover of
justices and constitutional theory would be assured.
Corwin steadily rejected other remedies. He dismissed

proposed constitutional amendments as slow and undemocratic, and he brushed aside with hardly a comment the
idea that Congress should expand the Court, allowing
Roosevelt to appoint new justices of his own tempera-
ment. Attorney General Homer Cummings sought Corwin's
opinions on the Court problems through much of 1936.
Cummings even advanced some of the Professor's pertinent
articles to the president in December of that year--while
Roosevelt vacationed in South America. Corwin was probably still not privy to the real plan brewing in the White
House.15

Corwin mentioned the "Court-packing" concept early
in his writings and never thought much of it. He wrote
in 1926 that a feature of the "working compromise" between having a weak or a strong Supreme Court was that
"Congress will not, at least in any but the gravest
cases, 'swamp' the Court in order to overcome an unwel-
come decision," and as late as January 1937 he continued
writing against the notion. On February 5 of that year
the president announced exactly what Corwin disliked:
Roosevelt sent to Congress a bill asking to expand the
Court to permit a new appointee for each justice who
did not retire at age seventy, up to a maximum total
of fifteen justices. Putting aside his recent and steady
opinions, Edward Corwin launched immediate and outspoken
support for Court-packing.16

His instant reversal came under heavy scrutiny. "When
I first saw the New York Times with the headlines
announcing it I was a bit startled," he later confessed.
"On further reflection I became convinced that the President has grasped the realities of the situation."
Corwin was speaking at Emory University in Atlanta when
Court-packing hit the newspapers. The questions came
quickly, and Corwin had ready opinions: "It is absurd
that the processes of government should be held up to
the extent that they have been by the Federal Courts."
He further talked down ideas that Court-packing represented dictatorship. Corwin was clearly a Roosevelt
loyalist.17

A Court-packing endorsement made good sense for
Corwin. The plan seemed to fulfill his model of reduced
judicial review together with popular legislation and
strong presidential leadership. The plan also increased
Corwin's prospects for joining the Court. Roosevelt
could make six new Court appointments, and with those
odds Corwin might have been an obvious choice. Corwin
also might have indirectly contributed to Roosevelt's
proposal during his service in Washington. While he
opposed Court-packing in his publications, his correspondence revealed light approval. Professor Arthur N.
Holcombe of Harvard University suggested a similar scheme
in a letter of December 7, 1936, and Corwin replied:
"I think your suggestion is most ingenious, devilishly

so. Nor is it altogether without legislative precedent. . . . I'm going to pass the idea along, and we'll
see what comes of it." His writings also uniquely linked
mandatory retirement with the need for fresh appointees
on the high Court. The concept was a fundamental part
of Court-packing, although in a different form. Corwin
probably had little more to do with developing Roosevelt's plan. A former Corwin student in the Justice
Department wrote to his mentor just days after the president's announcement to describe the plan's secret inception. The correspondent left no clue that Corwin might
have been part of the planning, but he did assure the
Princeton sage that he was a contender for the Court.[18]
    On March 17, 1937 the Senate Judiciary Committee
called Corwin before a hearing on Court-packing. A Senate panel was an ideal challenge for Professor Corwin.
The Senators would be his students as in a preceptor
"conference" from his early days at Princeton. He could
listen to comments and fire rapid questions in socratic
fashion to draw the "students" toward his way of thinking. A Senate panel would also offer Corwin a chance
to prove his mettle before the public and the president.
Showing his constitutional stuff would enhance chances
for the "big appointment" that hovered in his hopes.
Fourteen Senators and one Congressman awaited his appearance in Washington, as did reporters from major newspapers. All listened patiently while Corwin essayed
his belief that Roosevelt was within his power to propose
restructuring the Court, but soon came the questions.
Corwin was at the mercy of interrogators.[19]
    Senator Edward R. Burke, a Democrat from Nebraska,
drilled the issue of Corwin's changed views. He looked
back on the Professor's conclusion from the past year
that the "Court is already large enough" and asked blunt-
ly whether Corwin was reversing "that doctrine." Corwin
hedged. He belabored the point of whether he had fully
studied the matter. The Senator's question came back
in a different form: he asked the witness whether he
expected readers to rely on his statements, even with
the changes. Corwin could only say "yes." The integrity
of his writings and theories was on the spot. Burke
then turned to Corwin's writings on judicial review from
1914 and looked for differences from Corwin's current
stands. Mimicking the proposal that justices retire
at age seventy, Burke apologized for Corwin's later
views, noting that the scholar was "older, and weakening,
apparently, in . . . faculties." Corwin shot back:
"Have you got anything there I wrote when I was 6 years
old?" Little of the session was so tense. Corwin was
on stage. He commanded the proceedings with encyclopedic
explanations of constitutional law and history. He shot
down the Senators' statements with blunt answers, calling
one remark "bunk." When Corwin used the word "hermen-

eutics," he was asked to spell it. "Now, wait; is that fair?" he joked, but the Professor complied successfully. The hearing was also exhausting. It began at 10:30 that morning and lasted three hours.[20]

His performance under pressure was careful, scholarly, and well-prepared. Corwin captured the enthusiasm of most reporters, but he did not sell the president's plan to the Senators, and selling was his principal duty. The merits of Court-packing did not dominate the hearing; the session primarily reviewed the Professor's political flexibility. "I live and learn," he admitted about his changed theories. The reaction at Princeton was mixed. Students applauded "the General's" willingness to admit mistakes from his earlier years. Alumni, however, showed outrage. Some even questioned Corwin's faith in the honor code and other traditional Princeton values.[21]

Corwin was largely alone among intellectuals on the entire subject. Harold W. Dodds, the president of Princeton University, called Roosevelt's plan "the most startling evidence to date of the existence of a temper for absolutism in the White House." Corwin's own mentor, Professor McLaughlin, called Court-packing "a shocking disregard of elementary constitutional principles." Professor Corwin was also not pursuasive with his academic colleagues. Little more than two weeks before his Senate appearance, Corwin chaired a committee of lawyers and professors at the Brookings Institution on the Court-packing issue. The committee included distinguished attorneys Dean Acheson and Thuman Arnold and Professors Charles E. Clark, Robert E. Cushman, and Charles Grove Haines. Despite Corwin's leadership, the panel soundly condemned the president's plan for the Court. Corwin seemed to have no influence at all on the committee or its report.[22]

The intellectual community, a good share of the public, the president, and Congress supported New Deal legislation, but virtually no one backed Court-packing. It was perfectly constitutional for Congress to adjust the Court's composition. The plan's problem, however, was its blatant political inroads into the judiciary, violating the Court's independence and the separation of powers. Roosevelt's timing was also political. The Supreme Court had been an issue in the recent election, but the president saved the packing proposal and the criticism it generated until shortly after his re-election. The public and Congress could not support abrasive tampering with the Supreme Court. The public nevertheless wanted a change on the Court, and in April of 1937 the Court acceded to popular pressures by upholding the constitutionality of the Wagner Labor Relations Act. The New Deal was finally becoming solid law. Court-packing faded with welcome haste.[23]

The controversy was not over for Corwin. He failed as an advocate for reasons beyond the quality of the issue. He encountered three fundamental problems. First, his changed views of Court-packing were obvious and damaging to his credibility. Like the minor matter of the Supreme Court doors, Corwin found secondary concerns overshadowing the principal point. The Senators and reporters were more interested in a changed opinion than the real issue at hand. Second, his changed opinion was probably politically motivated. He was building to the pinnacle of his career, looking forward to working with the president and earning appointment to the Court. Moreover, the president's plan itself enhanced Corwin's chances for a judicial spot. Self-interest might have been evident. Third, Corwin sometimes lost the focus of his own arguments. When he spoke of Court-packing, he usually added arguments for mandatory retirement at age seventy and similar reform measures. At the Senate hearings he recommended that the Supreme Court be divided into three panels of five justices each. In a contemporary essay he concluded that a better plan would allow three new Court appointments during each presidential term. Without commitment to Court-packing he could not be convincing. Instead of reaching the pinnacle, Corwin followed a doomed issue.24

Corwin's role in the controversy brought added public attention, and the experience had profound negative consequences for him. It was an episode of deep personal, professional, and scholarly disappointment. Corwin wrote relatively little about the events, and he never gave the Court-packing threat much credit for persuading the justices to change their minds. "The essential thing," he concluded, "is that the Court did reconsider its position, thus putting itself in line with the rest of the government--back in the center of the tornado." He gave some warnings about the growing strength of presidential powers, and he continued to describe the era as a revolution in the structure of government and in popular perceptions of the Constitution. Corwin credited unions for compelling the Court's new posture. John L. Lewis led strikes and drew national attention to the need for the Wagner Act. The issue seemed to be over, but Corwin continued pushing for mandatory retirement of justices at age seventy or after twenty-one years on the bench.25

The following month brought the next step in the Supreme Court's New Deal history. Associate Justice Willis Van Devanter retired after twenty-seven years on the Court. Raymond Leslie Buell, a former Corwin student, carried to President Roosevelt the nomination of Edward Corwin for the justice's seat. With little suprise, the coveted offer went instead to Hugo Black. In the next two years, Roosevelt appointed Stanley Reed,

William Douglas, and Felix Frankfurter to the Court, and Corwin never gained serious consideration by the White House. He gambled his prospects on Court-packing. Its failure closed opportunities for the Professor and created a stigma. Much of his public notability resulted from association with the troubled proposal. Moreover, Corwin did not perform convincingly before the Senate; a Court nomination would bring confirmation hearings and more scrutiny by legislators, the public, and the press. Corwin could have become a burden to the administration.26

The disappointment closed the most important period in Corwin's career. His writings reached the public, the president sought his advice on constitutional matters, and the Professor was looking to join the Supreme Court. Instead, an unpopular scheme and an unproductive appearance in the Senate anchored him. Corwin remained a foremost constitutional scholar and political commentator, but the experiences ended his official ties with the Roosevelt administration. Indeed, Corwin began a campaign against many of the president's policies. His opposition grew in the succeeding years as the Supreme Court went clearly out of his reach and as international events replaced the New Deal in the news.

4

A New World
1938-1946

The Court-packing problems were a watershed for Edward Corwin. He was fully a public figure with all its appurtenant benefits and challenges. He was still the Professor of Jurisprudence at Princeton, but more of his time seemed to go toward writing and public appearances. Corwin regularly attended conferences and seminars, and he accepted appointments as a visiting professor at schools across the country. His role in the Supreme Court controversy did not cause much damage to his standing in the profession. But it followed him and changed the course of his political and academic pursuits and philosophies. The coming war in Europe gave the Professor a new subject of concern and a means of gracefully dropping support for Franklin Roosevelt.

Corwin saw the president's policies as leading the nation closer to war. He complimented passage of the Neutrality Act in 1939 as dispelling the "baleful and fatalistic conviction" of the administration that America must enter the war brewing in Europe. In the process of seeking neutrality, however, Congress delegated new powers to Roosevelt. Corwin cautiously accepted that trend. But when he examined the possibility of America's entry into the war, he noted that the powers passed to the president would "virtually convert the United States the moment it entered a war--any war at all, apparently into a totalitarian state." Rather than enlarging the president's powers in anticipation of world problems, wrote Corwin, "Let us see our war first!"[1]

Still, he generally approved of Congress's limited delegation of powers to Roosevelt. The Lend-Lease Act of March 11, 1941 changed his perception. Lend-Lease allowed the president to order production and delivery of arms and supplies for nations engaged in war. Roosevelt's new powers finally overstepped Corwin's limits.

To Corwin, Lend-Lease allowed the president to abandon collaboration with Congress and to invoke "the 'Commander-in-Chief' clause or some even vaguer theory of 'executive power' . . . to stake out Congress's course by a series of fait accomplis." Such behavior "must in the end have produced a serious constitutional crisis had not the Japanese obligingly come to the rescue." Lend-Lease also signalled the growth of presidential powers beyond those expressly delegated from Congress. In the 1940s Corwin introduced "the doctrine of inherent powers" to describe the phenomenon. He noted that if "the inherent-power theory" gained life before the war, "the delegated-power theory" in foreign relations was dead. The government's powers in that field were "so broad, so indefinite, so overlapping" that they were inseparable, and the powers must be separated before determining whether Congress had delegated a power or whether the president's authority were an "inherent power."2

The Princeton Professor had long studied the separation of powers in foreign affairs. In 1920, Corwin criticized Presidents William McKinley, Theodore Roosevelt, and Woodrow Wilson for using the military without congressional authorization, but when Franklin Roosevelt attempted similar actions, Corwin blamed Congress. Preceding World War Two, the president employed the navy to convoy British merchantships. With a strained approach, Corwin defended Congress's unused power to halt the convoys. Writing to the New York Times in February 1941 he highlighted Congress's power to control these "acts of hostility" against "Great Britain's enemies." The president must have flexibility to respond to emergencies, Corwin believed, but Congress must limit the forfeiture of its own powers. Corwin still attacked Roosevelt's "truly royal prerogative" in assuming vast authority.3

Corwin's interests in presidential powers culminated in 1940 with his publication of The President: Office and Powers. Corwin had studied the executive office in books and articles throughout his career, but his new tome was his first comprehensive examination of the presidency. He undertook an institutional analysis, isolating the president's roles--commander-in-chief, legislative leader, chief executive, and others. The Professor supported his text with numerous footnotes and historical background, in his customary scholarly style. The book renewed Corwin's reputation among the public and academics. His latest achievement would no longer be his lonely support for Court-packing. He was once again the Professor concentrating and dedicating himself to scholarship. He was stepping out of politics and into the arena of detachment and unbiased views. But the step was never complete. Corwin would always be the commentator. Thoughts about contemporary events ran throughout his writings. Court-packing lessons might have kept him from Washington, but they did not quiet the Professor's vigorous political commentary.4

Corwin signed the preface to The President on September 1, 1940, and the book included little about executive agreements; the next day Roosevelt livened the topic by announcing the Destroyer-Bases Agreement. Roosevelt made a sweeping executive agreement to exchange fifty destroyers for British military bases on the Atlantic Ocean. Corwin attacked Roosevelt's assumption of powers in a lengthy letter to the New York Times. He found the agreement unconstitutional on three points: Congress, not the president, had the exclusive right to dispose of American property; the agreement invaded Congress's right to define requirements of international law respecting neutrality; and the step toward belligerent status invaded Congress's power to declare war. Corwin criticized Roosevelt, but attacked Congress as well. The requirement that two-thirds of the Senate approve treaties for ratification compelled the president to use executive agreements. Moreover, circumstances often demanded prompt action, and Congress was rarely capable of such efficiency. The president could compensate for these deficiencies, wrote Corwin, by submitting the plan for congressional approval after the fact. Congress surely would have approved the popular agreement.5

In examining executive agreements, Corwin distinguished between agreements "carrying out a conceded executive power" and agreements "effectuating a power of Congress." The former were acceptable, but the latter infringed on congressional power. In a limited defense of the agreements, Corwin concluded, "even the most convinced critic of the executive agreement device would scarcely contend that the President ought to go to the Senate every time he finds it desirable to arrive at a common understanding with one of our allies regarding matters of military policy." The essence of Corwin's constitutional thought was that a strong president was necessary, but Congress must retain its powers. The Professor usually criticized the president when he usurped congressional powers, but Corwin blamed Congress most heavily for acquiescing.6

The end of Franklin Roosevelt's second term brought other events for Corwin's examination. Congressional delegation of powers allowed the creation of new federal agencies. Corwin reluctantly approved the agencies and their control by the president. Corwin distinguished, however, between agencies created by Congress and agencies "summoned into existence by the magic wand of the President without reference to statutory authorization." He objected to Roosevelt's 1939 reorganization plan, because the president was bringing under his control agencies established outside the executive branch. Corwin feared that agency-president relations would parallel cabinet-president relations: "unqualified dominion on the one hand and . . . complete subordination on the other."[7]

Corwin's study of presidential powers revolved around his theory of the "aggrandized presidency." Writing in 1917, the Professor indicated that the president had special powers in foreign affairs, but his duties and Congress's powers damped them. Seven years later, he cautiously observed that "it may be fairly said that the history of presidential power has been one of aggrandizement." Presidential aggrandization was finally in full effect from the beginning of Roosevelt's incumbency. Corwin was a Roosevelt supporter through the New Deal years, and he backed the flow of powers toward the president through most of the 1930s. Corwin's late opposition to the president's policies then came to a test in the 1940 election. Roosevelt was running for a third term, and Wendell Willkie was the Republican nominee.[8]

Professor Corwin long opposed a third term for presidents. No president before Roosevelt held three terms, and in 1927 Corwin told a reporter, "limiting the president's term of office to eight years is an understanding which has become a part of our constitutional system." He warned about the two-term tradition: "to discard it would be dangerous." Corwin kept that danger in mind when he voted for Roosevelt in 1936. An advantage of giving him a second term was that he would not be "thinking of another term in the White House. . . ." Roosevelt proved Corwin wrong. In the 1940 election Corwin cited the two-term tradition as his primary reason for supporting Willkie. Corwin also wrote harshly of Roosevelt's foreign policy, his alienation of business, and his political tactics. "Finally, I am going to vote for Mr. Willkie," emphasized the Professor, "because I feel that Mr. Roosevelt has shot his bolt. He did an excellent job in the first five years of his incumbency, getting some long-overdue legislative reforms enacted and established on a firm constitutional basis, but he has done his work and should now step down." Corwin still had kind words for the New Deal and the constitutional "revolution," but for little else about the president.[9]

A sense of disappointment and frustration touched Corwin's statements about the 1940 election. He wrote of Roosevelt's using foreign policy to distract attention from the discovery that Hugo Black, Roosevelt's first appointee to the Supreme Court, was a former Ku Klux Klan member. Early the next year he spoke critically of all Roosevelt appointees to the Court without supporting the charges.10 He only begged suspicions about his own disappointment in not getting the top position himself. Corwin offered several reasons for opposing Roosevelt, but he had only narrow reasons for favoring Willkie. He called Willkie's policies regarding unemployment and the federal deficit "optimistic and vigorous," while Roosevelt's were "weak and despairing." Willkie, moreover, held the confidence of business concerns. Corwin might have found one more reason for supporting the Republican. In The President: Office and Powers, Corwin proposed a new form of cabinet comprising leading members of Congress. He wanted to link the president and Congress to provide for greater coordination and improved relationships between the branches. The notion attracted academic attention, but it had little likelihood of being realized. A month before the election, however, Raymond Buell sent a personal letter to Corwin declaring, "One reason I am hopeful of Mr. Willkie's election is because I think he might try out your idea of a different type of Cabinet. . . ." Roosevelt was certainly not going to give Corwin another role in the government, but perhaps Willkie would. Roosevelt, of course, won a third term. That term brought even further expansion of presidential powers and America's entry into World War Two.11

Roosevelt and Congress gained unprecedented powers during the New Deal and pre-war years, but America's entry into World War Two allowed Roosevelt to assume many more powers as the nation's commander-in-chief. Corwin continued his criticism of the president, although he usually blamed Congress when the balance of power shifted too far toward Roosevelt. The Emergency Price Control Act confrontation clearly illustrated the Professor's theory. Roosevelt warned that if Congress did not repeal a portion of the Act, he would assume the power to disregard Congress's decision. Corwin acknowledged that presidents had occasionally considered themselves not obligated to Congress when it "trenched on Presidential prerogatives," but Roosevelt's message went beyond those precedents. Congress was perfectly within its rights to pass or not to pass the Emergency Price Control Act.12

Corwin admonished that the power Roosevelt threatened to use was beyond presidential scope, even under "the inherent-power theory." When Congress followed the president's wishes, Corwin blamed Congress for permitting Roosevelt's misperceptions. Congress needed to improve its organization and procedures before it could gather sufficient popular support to resist a president in time of war. The Emergency Price Control Act also compelled the Professor to re-examine the Supreme Court's future in presidential-congressional relations and powers. The New Deal signalled "the twi-

light of the Supreme Court" and the decline of judicial
review. But the growth of presidential power and the
Emergency Price Control Act inspired a new, short-lived
prediction: "I suggest that the time may not be distant
when the Court will once more achieve greatness, to wit,
as a balancing agency between Congress and the president. Thus will judicial review, like the eagle, renew
its youth. . . ." The hope was never fulfilled, and
judicial review met further decline. The Court generally would not interrupt emergency actions or political
disputes, so the president was "accountable only by his
own conscience."13

The further decline of judicial review and of congressional powers led Corwin to search for ways to revive
Congress's role in the government. In the late 1930s
Congress began using concurrent resolutions to limit
delegation of powers. Congress allowed the president
to exercise certain powers, but a resolution opposing
particular actions would terminate them. Known in later
years as "legislative vetoes," Corwin gave them little
attention before 1940. When concurrent resolutions became more prevalent in wartime legislation, he praised
them as allowing "Congress and the President needed
elbowroom in dealing with the complexities of modern
industrial life." Concurrent resolutions permitted the
distinction between abdication and delegation of powers.
Their constitutionality was also in question, but Corwin
rejected arguments against them; he believed that an
act of Congress could be made to terminate upon any given
event, including subsequent action by either or both
houses of Congress.14

The president still found other means of expanding
powers during World War Two. Roosevelt's control of
"war-agencies" was to Corwin the most remarkable development of the president's legislative power. Agency
developments and other federal actions during the war
enhanced Corwin's aggrandized presidency theory. The
president also gained authority as an international
leader. "As head of the principal military power of
the free world he provides leadership to a half dozen
military alliances around the globe," wrote the Professor. The president's aggrandized powers--all controlled
by one individual--meant that executive acts could be
highly personalized. Writing in 1940, Corwin discerned
that presidential power and prestige represented America's "most valuable political asset," although he feared
their implications. Unduly personalized powers invited
two dangers: "antagonism between president and Congress
and autocracy." After the experiences of total war,
however, Corwin expanded his outlook. The breakdown
of wartime interbranch relations demonstrated that unduly
personalized powers invited two slightly different dan-

gers: "the slowing down of the legislative process to an extent that unfits it for a crisis-ridden world in which time is often of the essence, and--in consequence-- autocracy."15

The war years also brought Roosevelt's re-election to a fourth term. Corwin was still critical about the third term, so the fourth came with pointed remarks. A reporter asked about a fourth term more than a year before the election, and Corwin chuckled sarcastically when he spoke of Roosevelt: "Well, considering the shape in which the country may very well be at the end of the third term, I don't think he deserves anything better." The Professor told the same reporter that John L. Lewis was "a creation of Mr. Roosevelt," and that labor must be called upon to make sacrifices. Corwin affirmed his support for the New Deal, but he attacked the labor leader who organized strikes leading to the Supreme Court's endorsement of the New Deal reforms. He was isolating the New Deal from the later events of Roosevelt's incumbency. Roosevelt won his fourth term, and Corwin claimed in disgust that Americans were "hood-winked" into electing "a very sick man."16

The 1940s also brought Edward Corwin's final years as the McCormick Professor of Jurisprudence. January 19, 1946 was his sixty-eighth birthday, and Corwin had reached retirement age. White hair showed his age, but Corwin's personal strength and professional ambition belied his years. The coming years offered numerous visiting professorships, ample opportunity for prolific writing, and winter vacations in Florida. Corwin's retirement was also something of a milestone for Princeton University. Corwin was one of three original preceptors retiring in spring of 1946, and they were the last of the charter "preceptor guys." That fact and Corwin's popular acclaim brought banquets and news coverage to the occasion. Time magazine mentioned the events and briefly described Edward Corwin as a Court-packing supporter. The New Deal was inescapable.17

Corwin's role in the New Deal and Court-packing issues was essential for understanding Corwin in the 1940s. His opposition to Roosevelt was more than the fact that he was "born a Republican" and favored a two-term limit on the presidency. Corwin changed from a strong supporter of Franklin Roosevelt to someone who could find virtually nothing good in the president's economic policies, foreign policies, congressional relations, and Supreme Court appointees. The president did indeed change in the late 1930s as he gathered increased powers and shifted attention from the economic crisis toward the world war. But Corwin's shift was nearly complete. Even when he spoke of the New Deal, his support seemed belabored and contrived. Corwin also shifted his academic pursuits in part. His principal studies centered on the presidency rather than on the judiciary. Just as the 1930s shaped Corwin for the 1940s, the directions he set for himself during World War Two remained the course he would pursue in the next decade.

5
The Princeton Sage
1946-1963

Diversity and specialization characterized Edward Corwin's career. He concentrated his energies on constitutional law and history, but he examined the myriad of topics and issues the fields touched. The retirement years brought a new balance. Corwin maintained his dedication and concentration, but he reached for new fields, and he gave his talents and knowledge fresh practical applications that did not bear the risks of tampering with the Supreme Court. Amidst the business of retirement he was still "the General" at Princeton and "Professor Corwin" at a wide range of schools. Edward and Mildred Corwin became avid travelers. Corwin brought his "Constitutional Interpretation" course to schools across the nation, and he presented major lectures at the University of Michigan, Claremont College, and other institutions. He also remained in the news as the reliable spokesman on virtually every political subject.

The last years of the 1940s began a period for Corwin best described by his most important projects and interests. His pursuits were largely successful during that era, and he was even called for a bit of government service. The Secretary of the Air Force employed the retired professor for several days in April of 1948 at the standard daily rate of fifty dollars. The pay was moderate, and the scope of his duties was not specified, but the invitation from Washington must have been enthusiastically received. Corwin always accepted calls from Washington, and he had not gained one in a decade. His most significant Washington duty began in 1949 as he led a project in the Library of Congress to draft an annotated and interpretive guide to the United States Constitution. The resulting tome, published in 1953, immediately became a fundamental resource for all aspects of constitutional law. Corwin never wrote the comprehensive study of the Constitution he planned, but the Library of Congress publication nearly satisfied that ambition. With its thousand pages of documented analysis, the book was a sweeping account of contemporary constitutional law and its historical development. It was the perfect hornbook.[1]

Not all concerns were as productive and optimistic. Corwin remained the critical observer of the Supreme Court, and he increasingly rejected the direction of modern law. The Court ruled in 1948 that public schools could not offer "released time" for students to engage in religious activities of their own choosing. Even though the schools were not advocating particular religious affiliation, the conduct still violated the First Amendment's separation of church and state. Corwin found the decision ludicrous. Arguing in public lectures and scholarly articles, he asserted that the First Amendment only prohibited discrimination in favor of a religious preference. "Released time" was not discriminatory and thus should be constitutional. Corwin had no church affiliation, but his usual outspoken manner won instant admiration from church groups condemning the Court ruling. The Catholic press especially adored the man. America, a weekly Catholic magazine, recited Corwin's credentials as a colleague of Woodrow Wilson and author of treatises on constitutional law when it heralded the Professor's attacks on the Supreme Court. The church was not accustomed to such strong and independent intellectual backing.[2]

The Princeton Professor and the Catholic church found compatriots in one another. In a private letter to the editor of America in 1950, Corwin supported federal funding for parochial schools: "although I am not at all a religious person, I still retain enough early piety to resent the idea, which is so entirely false historically, that the Constitution does not countenance aid to religion in any form."[3] His most salient tie with the church came late the next year when President Harry Truman proposed sending an ambassador to the Vatican. Many Catholics in the United States endorsed the move, but most Americans raised objections. Separation of church and state was again at issue. Corwin sided with Truman. He tackled the issue with articles and a letter in the New York Times flatly declaring that Truman was acting within his constitutional powers to control foreign affairs, and that the decision was unchallengeable by any means. This time the Professor's comments swept the Catholic press. America and Catholic News gave him coverage, and Catholic Digest and Catholic Mind reprinted excerpts from the Corwin letter. Edward Corwin might not have been a religious person, but he was a special spokesman for an array of religious issues. He also seemed undeterred by being on the losing end of each issue; Truman never appointed the ambassador, and released time remained unconstitutional.[4]

The Catholic issues revealed Corwin's growing conservativism. He was the liberal intellectual from his early years at Princeton through the New Deal. But his estrangement from the Roosevelt administration after the Court-packing controversy instilled a seed of conservative philosophy. The seed nurtured during World War Two on issues of presidential power and international relations. By the early 1950s, the conservative streak ran through social issues. Corwin had been a reliable social liberal. For decades he advocated greater government participation in social matters, and he favored the New Deal's reformative effects. The Catholic issues showed that Corwin did not favor a strict separation of church and state. That position, however, might not have been a drastic change for Corwin on the subject of First Amendment civil liberties. He had long espoused a narrow perspective on free speech rights.[5]

Corwin's moderate conservativism also reflected in his opinion of the landmark Brown v. Board of Education case. A unanimous Supreme Court ruled in May 1954 that segregation in public schools was unconstitutional. The case pointedly rejected the "separate but equal" doctrine and sent school districts throughout the nation toward integration. Corwin's public statements were moderate. He did not agree when the Court declared segregated schools to be inherently unequal; instead, he called segregation the parent of inequality. That formula could possibly tolerate some segregation, although Corwin did not openly confess it. He also argued for slow implementation of integration enforcement.[6] Corwin's confidants heard a more blatant opinion. They understood the Professor to favor "separate but equal." Moreover, when the segregation issue touched his neighborhood, he gave the Court a mixed review. Local Princeton faculty circulated a "Covenant of Open Occupancy" in 1957 presumably stating that no person should be barred from home ownership in the neighborhood because of race. Corwin declined to sign. He wrote privately that the Brown holding was "sound" but based on a "very weak opinion" which ignored the purposes of the Equal Protection Clause. Corwin refused to bring the "desegregation doctrine into nongovernmental areas. . . ." He then closed the letter in a revealing and unusually non-legalistic manner: "I am frank to say that I should not myself think of selling my home to colored folk without first consulting my adjoining neighbors, and I should expect the same consideration from them."[7]

The liberal spirit of earlier decades surfaced briefly in the 1950s. Corwin became a leader for the defense of the "Trenton Six," a group of black men sentenced to death in New Jersey's capital amidst a mood of racism and persecution. Prosecutors brought the charges after the murder of an elderly white man in Trenton. Weak evidence against the six defendants brought the case wide publicity, and the National Association for the Advancement of Colored People and the Communist Party joined forces to defend the accused. Edward Corwin seemed an unlikely sympathizer. He did not oppose the death penalty, and he was not an ardent civil rights proponent. Yet he found himself leading a group destined to take charge of the Trenton Six defense. Professor Corwin and Francis J. McConnell, a Methodist bishop, chaired the Princeton Committee for Defense of the Trenton Six. The committee comprised only twenty-seven members, but it removed the Communist Party from the case and installed the American Civil Liberties Union to work with the NAACP. The change was probably a practical move as well as a public relations improvement. The New Jersey Supreme Court soon ordered a new trial; four of the defendants were then acquitted and two received life sentences. The state's high court ultimately reversed those two convictions. Corwin and his fellow committee members endured bitter reactions. Republican leaders asked Princeton University to order its professors out of the case, and the whole group tolerated threatening letters.[8]

The episode was an anomaly for Edward Corwin. He was engaged with some of the country's most prominent liberal or radical organizations and was taking a close role in a criminal proceeding. Corwin often expressed unpopular opinions, and he had worked on several legal proceedings, but never had his efforts so closely involved the civil rights and the guilt or innocence of individuals on trial. Contributing a constitutional theory to an appellate brief lacks the immediacy of watching young men, perhaps innocent, be sent to the electric chair. The case was more than a touch of liberalism for a retired septuagenarian. It showed Corwin's willingness to try new and bold ventures and to contend with intense criticism.

Corwin must have liked the experience. In 1953 he accepted the co-chairmanship of another committee destined to generate more sharp opposition. But this committee would focus directly on the issues of constitutional powers that the Professor had studied throughout his career. Senator John Bricker, an Ohio Republican, introduced in Congress a constitutional amendment intended to curtail the president's treaty-making powers. The "Bricker Amendment" prohibited all executive agreements and any treaties that infringed on the police powers of states or violated pre-existing federal statutes. Corwin had been writing about treaty powers since his first book in 1913. He had also written on the need to curb presidential powers. Bricker designed his amendment to do that curbing, but it did not satisfy Corwin. Criticism of the aggrandized presidency did not deter Corwin's long endorsement of extensive treaty powers. He urged President Wilson in 1913 to use his treaty powers to resolve Japanese relations in California. He accepted executive agreements during World War Two, even though Franklin Roosevelt used his authority to make the broad Destroyer-Bases Agreement. Corwin might have wanted to restrict the aggrandized presidency, but not the treaty powers.9

"The Committee for Defense of the Constitution by Preserving the Treaty Power" came into existence in late 1953 with Corwin, General Lucius D. Clay, and John W. Davis as the co-chairmen. Davis had been the Democratic presidential nominee in 1924. A new version of the Amendment was in the Senate and heading for passage. Dwight Eisenhower was in the White House, and he had not yet announced a position on the issue. Opponents needed to act quickly. Eisenhower was a newcomer in Washington, and he held informal "stag dinners" to become more closely acquainted with prominent men in government. In December 1953, the stag party invitation list conveniently included Corwin, Clay, and Davis. Eisenhower greeted Corwin and Clay as they arrived together. Clay stepped away to a telephone call, leaving the Princeton Professor alone with the president of the United States. Corwin was then seventy-five years old, gaining a bit of weight, and showing his age with thinning white hair. He was alone with an incumbent president for probably the only time in his life.10

Small talk took its usual course. Corwin complimented a painting in the room, and Eisenhower told of receiving it from Konrad Adenauer. "He asked me for one of mine in return," laughed the amateur artist. The few moments alone either allowed an eased relationship or provided time for persuasive comments. The evening brought the three leading public opponents of the Bricker Amendment together with the president, Attorney General Herbert Brownell, and Under Secretary of State Walter Bedell Smith. The next month Eisenhower announced his unalterable opposition to Bricker's proposals. The amendment failed by one vote in the Senate. Corwin described the evening: "That was the time we finished off Bricker."11

Corwin and Eisenhower met only once, but Corwin had further involvement with the administration. The Professor admired Eisenhower from his early months in office. He excused the president's early problems as the result of relative inexperience with the ways of Washington, although he lightly criticized the appointment of "nine millionaires" to the cabinet.12 Eisenhower's shortcomings, according to Corwin, were compensated by the selection of Richard Nixon as vice president. Corwin spent spring of 1954 as a visiting professor at Whittier College in California, Nixon's alma mater. In an article he wrote from lectures at the school, Corwin suggested a more prominent position for the vice president. "The first care of the head of a great corporation," analogized the commentator, "is to take thought of a possible successor and to set him on a course of training. That very idea--who can doubt it--has also presented itself to the President's mind in his effort to enable Mr. Nixon to earn his salary. We can be glad that he has such good material to work upon."13

Nixon learned of Corwin's remarks, and the Professor and the vice president became occasional correspondents. "This is just a note to thank you for your very generous comments regarding me," wrote Nixon. The two men met years later at a dinner meeting of the Academy of Political Science, and Corwin handed Nixon an autographed copy of his complimentary Whittier article. The humbling admiration came again in a personal letter signed by "Dick Nixon:" "May I tell you again that as a Whittier graduate and a history major I am very proud of the fact that a scholar of your great reputation and stature chose to come to our small institution as a visiting professor."14

Nixon's importance in the Eisenhower administration accelerated during the president's illnesses and heart attack. The events tested constitutional procedures for presidential disability. The vice president was obviously the successor upon the president's death, but what happens when the chief executive is disabled? When is the president unfit to hold office, and who makes that decision? The questions riddled the press and Congress. Corwin stood prepared with his answers. He suggested legislative action to resolve uncertainties. Corwin envisaged creation of a review panel to determine the president's ability to hold office and his return to power after temporary disabilities. The Constitution was not clear on the issues, but Congress could establish guides.15

The late 1950s began to slow the ambitious professor. Opportunities continued, but he was turning many down. Illnesses kept him from congressional hearings, and the Professor declined the invitation to draft a new constitution for the nation of Vietnam.16 Subsequent events surely would have eradicated Corwin's constitution, but in 1955 the invitation must have been flattering and tempting. Corwin did accept a four-year appointment in 1956 to the committee administering the Oliver Wendell Holmes devise, but he apparently had little role in the Supreme Court history it sponsored. An operation and medical diet in the next year prevented his contribution to a book marking the retirement of Professor Robert Cushman. His colleagues were not used to seeing Corwin turn down projects, and Clinton Rossiter wrote to his former mentor with a tone of encouragement, astonishment, and sympathy: "I am grieved that you cannot go ahead with the intended subject. It would have been a most important contribution to the book, and I really think you are underestimating your emotional capacity in this matter. That, however, is much easier for me to say than you to agree with."17

January 19, 1958 was Edward Corwin's eightieth birthday. The slowness of age and the burdens of illnesses began to keep Edward and Mildred at home. They moved at the time of his retirement to a rustic and smaller house a mile or more from the Princeton University campus. It was a landmark edifice known as "Old Stone House" for its rock walls measuring up to two feet thick. The ancient structure offered a perfect historical mood. It also had a private study on the second floor with windows admitting bright sun and warmth. There the aged professor maintained his scholarship and dedication to constitutional law. Longhand notes covered two card tables as he prepared the twelfth edition of The Constitution and What It Means Today. The last years of the 1950s brought a few more book reviews and letters to editors. The usual zeal continued as he condemned the Warren Court's "weird" rulings.18

Corwin's final publication appeared in 1960. He was eighty-two and beginning a brief period of true, complete retirement. Friends from the university paid cordial visits; former students sent letters of admiration and well-wishes. The complete lack of publications in the later years evidenced the burden of Corwin's illnesses. For a man with twenty books to his credit, as well as hundreds of essays, letters to editors, and book reviews, complete silence seemed impossible. Mildred and Edward were aging together and nearly alone. They never had children, and their few close relatives were back in Michigan. The university and its personal and professional friendships were the mainstay of their lives. Harold Dodds, Princeton's former president, looked after the Corwins with obedience and care. In April 1963 Dodds knew that Corwin was suffering his last illness. He made some final preparations, uncertain whether "the General" would live a week or a year. Edward Corwin died on April 29 at Princeton Hospital at age eighty-five. Mildred Corwin lived until 1969.19

Corwin left a permanent legacy at Princeton University and on the study of constitutional law and history. His writings became an essential part of twentieth century law. His teaching shaped the study of the Constitution at Princeton and at universities across the country. He was Woodrow Wilson's successor, but he

contributed far more to classroom teaching than Wilson
ever could amidst his administrative responsibilities
and political ambitions. Princeton honored Corwin by
renaming the Politics Department building from Wilson
Hall to Corwin Hall. Alpheus Thomas Mason became the
fourth McCormick Professor of Jurisprudence upon Corwin's
retirement. Mason continued the historical tradition
of study that Wilson and Corwin adopted. Walter F.
Murphy followed Mason and transformed "Con Interp" into
a quantitative and comparative course; "political science" displaced the historical perspectives that Wilson,
Corwin, and Mason highlighted.20 Just as time left Corwin's teaching methods behind, the years diminished the
contemporary usefulness of many of his writings. Other
professors kept The Constitution and What It Means Today
and Understanding the Constitution current with new editions. Only The President: Office and Powers remains
widely used among Corwin's original publications, but
even the 1957 edition is subject to modern revision.
Corwin never wrote the comprehensive constitutional tome
he planned. Instead, he wrote for his time. Virtually
all of his publications responded to contemporary events
from the League of Nations to the Warren Court. He
seemed to prefer the excitement of modern commentary
to the merits of making a permanent landmark in scholarship. His writings therefore survive for their historical interest and as examples of a professor's dedication
to studying, teaching, and commenting on all aspects
of American government.

Part Two
Bibliography of
Edward S. Corwin

Introduction

The bibliography of Edward S. Corwin comprises more than 400 citations to publications by Corwin and 225 references to publications about the Professor. The writings in this bibliography are arranged chronologically within their respective categories: Books Written by Corwin; Books Edited by Corwin; Parts of Books Written by Corwin; Articles Written by Corwin; "Letters to the Editor" Written by Corwin; Book Reviews Written by Corwin; and Writings About Corwin. Each book of which Corwin was a co-author, such as The Presidency Today (Entry A20), is credited here as a "Book Written by Corwin," because his contributions are not identifiably separate from the contributions of his collaborator, Louis Koenig. The few articles on which Corwin shared authorship are similarly listed under "Articles Written by Corwin" (Entries D158 and D182). Each bibliographical entry is catalogued with a letter corresponding to its category and with a number indicating its place within the category. Entry numbers of books with multiple editions include a decimal number. Entry A12.3, for example, indicates the third edition of the twelfth book in the "Books Written by Corwin" category.

Other aspects of the bibliography are detailed as follows:

1. Citation Forms. The bibliography generally adheres to The Chicago Manual of Style (13th edition) with significant variations for clarity and completeness and to comply with the author's preferred style. For example, newspaper and encyclopedia citations include authors and other details. All dates appear in the traditional style of "July 4, 1776," rather than as "4 July 1776." Citations consequently use the "pp."

abbreviation for "pages" to set the page numbers apart from the numbers in dates.

2. <u>Tense</u>. The annotations are generally written in the present tense, even when referring to past events. Present tense keeps the prose fresher and livelier and avoids the complexities of switching from present-tense descriptions of the publications themselves to past-tense descriptions of Corwin and his theories.

3. <u>Parts of Books</u>. This category includes Corwin's essays in independent volumes as distinguished from essays in periodicals. It also includes essays in books published as part of a series or set (e.g. Entry C14) or as proceedings of conferences or meetings (e.g. Entry C3).

4. <u>Articles</u>. This category includes not only Corwin's independent essays in periodicals, but also transcripts of his panel discussions (e.g. Entries D139 and D171) and his original statements as part of collections of independent comments on particular issues (e.g. Entries D88 and D140).

5. <u>Book Reviews</u>. Book titles and authors are as indicated in the published reviews; some discrepancies may therefore occur between the citations in the bibliography and the actual books themselves.

6. <u>Reprints</u>. Many publishers have issued reprints of Corwin's books, and many of Corwin's articles have been reprinted in books and other periodicals. Book reprints are noted immediately after the reprinted editions without independent entry numbers (e.g. Entries A1 and A5.2). Article reprints are generally listed separately with independent entry numbers. Publishers acknowledged the reprinted books as reprints, and the books usually carried the identical format as the originals; article reprints, however, were often held out as original publications. Reprints listed at Entries D55, D97, D119, D126, D150, and D167 do not have independent entry numbers. Those reprints do not possess the independent qualities characteristic of most other article reprints. Whenever a publication has been later reprinted, reference to the reprint appears immediately after the principal entry citation. Whenever an entry is itself a reprint, that fact is mentioned in the annotation.

7. <u>Foreign Publications</u>. Foreign publications appear in the bibliography only if written by Corwin and if original in content or form. The bibliography therefore includes Corwin's articles in Chinese journals (Entries

D69 and D70) and his one French essay (Entry D143).
Not included are simultaneous publications by British
or Canadian presses and translations of Corwin's books
into German, Spanish, Portuguese, Korean, and other
languages.

8. <u>Unpublished Material</u>. Only one unpublished item
appears in the bibliography--Gerald Garvey's doctoral
dissertation listed at Entry G200. Opening the bibliography to unpublished works would give the project an
unmanageable scope, but Garvey's dissertation is included
because of its importance and availability from University Microfilms.

9. <u>Chronology</u>. All entries within each category
are listed in chronological order, except as necessary
to keep related articles together, as at Entries D103-
D112.

10. <u>Typography</u>. The citations in this bibliography
generally adhere to the capitalization and punctuation
as used in the original publication cited. Thus, some
inconsistencies and irregularities may occur (e.g. Entry
G124). Clear errors are corrected. For example, the
original book review listed at Entry F102 uses the word
"treatises" where "treaties" was obviously intended.

11. <u>Dates of Inclusion</u>. The cut-off date of the
bibliography is June 1, 1984. The lists of publications
by Corwin are generally limited to the years of Corwin's
life, except for collections of Corwin essays (Entries
A21-A23) and certain reprints of his essays listed under
"Parts of Books Written by Corwin" (Entries C29-C30).
Not included are editions of Corwin's books revised and
prepared by other authors after Corwin's death (see
references at Entries A6 and A17).

A
Books Written by Corwin

A1   National Supremacy: Treaty Power vs. State
Power. New York: Henry Holt and Company,
1913.

       Reprint: Gloucester, Mass.: Peter Smith,
               1965.

    Reviews the constitutional relationship between the
state and federal governments and analyzes sources of
federal supremacy over states. Corwin isolates those
powers reserved for states and those for the federal
government, then examines conflicts and judicial opinions related to such powers. He concludes that "the
treaty power of the United States is not constitutionally
restricted by the police powers of the states. . . ."
See Entry E5.

A2   The Doctrine of Judicial Review: Its Legal
and Historical Basis and Other Essays. Princeton: Princeton University Press, 1914.

       Reprints: Entry C12 (Chapter 1 only); and
               Gloucester, Mass.: Peter Smith,
               1963.

    Collects five essays, including revisions of the
articles listed at Entries D11, D13, and D15. Other
essays examine the origin of the Constitution as a compact among the people rather than among the states and
the relationship between states' rights and federal
treaty-making power.

A3   French Policy and the American Alliance of 1778. Princeton: Princeton University Press, 1916.

         Reprints: Hamden, Conn.: Archon Books, 1962; Gloucester, Mass.: Peter Smith, 1962 and 1969; and New York: Burt Franklin, 1970.

Surveys the relationship between France and the United States during the American Revolution. The book is expanded from Corwin's doctoral dissertation (Ph.D. diss., University of Pennsylvania, 1905). Chapters 1 and 2 are reprinted from the article listed at Entry D19.

A4   The President's Control of Foreign Relations. Princeton: Princeton University Press, 1917.

         Reprints: New York: Johnson Reprint Corporation, 1970; and Ann Arbor, Mich.: University Microfilms, 1972.

Analyzes the scope of presidential authority in foreign affairs and outlines its historical development. Corwin separates foreign relations into three categories: diplomatic intercourse, treaties and executive agreements, and war-making powers. He reviews the historical development of foreign relations and concludes that the president "decisively and conspicuously" remains in control. See Entry E14.

A5.1   John Marshall and the Constitution: A Chronicle of the Supreme Court. Abraham Lincoln Edition. The Chronicles of America Series, vol. 16. New Haven: Yale University Press, 1919.

    A5.2   Textbook Edition. New Haven: Yale University Press, 1919.

         Reprint: New York: United States Publishers Association, 1977.

    A5.3   Graduates' Edition. New Haven: Yale University Press, 1920.

    A5.4   Extra-Illustrated Edition. New Haven: Yale University Press, 1920.

A5.5   Roosevelt Edition. New Haven: Yale University Press, 1921.

A5.6   Extra-Illustrated Edition. New Haven: Yale University Press, 1921.

A5.7   Textbook Edition. New Haven: Yale University Press, 1921.

Presents a general biography of Chief Justice John Marshall during the years he served on the United States Supreme Court. Corwin regards Marshall as the founder of American constitutional law. Although many of Marshall's decisions have been overruled, Corwin still emphasizes that the Chief Justice's theories shape modern Supreme Court rulings. See Entries C6 and G11.

A6.1   The Constitution and What It Means Today. Princeton: Princeton University Press, 1920.

A6.2   2nd ed. Princeton: Princeton University Press, 1921.

A6.3   3rd ed. Princeton: Princeton University Press, 1924.

A6.4   4th ed. Princeton: Princeton University Press, 1930.

A6.5   5th ed. Princeton: Princeton University Press, 1937.

A6.6   6th ed. Princeton: Princeton University Press, 1938.

A6.7   7th ed. Princeton: Princeton University Press, 1941.

A6.8   8th ed. Princeton: Princeton University Press, 1946.

A6.9   9th ed. Princeton: Princeton University Press, 1947.

A6.10   10th ed. Princeton: Princeton University Press, 1948.

A6.11   11th ed. Princeton: Princeton University Press, 1954.

A6.12   12th ed. Princeton: Princeton University Press, 1958.

Analyzes the contemporary meaning and interpretations of each clause of the United States Constitution. The book reprints each clause, then presents textual analyses supported by citations to statutes and cases. The analyses include historical interpretations, commentary on Supreme Court rulings, and clear explanations of every term in the Constitution from "United States" to "due process." Harold W. Chase and Craig R. Ducat have prepared 1973 and 1978 editions of the book, with some annual supplements.

A7   The President's Removal Power Under the Constitution. National Municipal League Monograph Series. New York: National Municipal League, 1927.

Revised and expanded from the article listed at Entry D68.

A8   The Democratic Dogma and the future of Political Science and other essays. Yenching Political Science Series. Shanghai: Kelly & Walsh, Limited, 1930.

Reprint: Entry A23 (Chapter 4 only).

Collects four essays, including revisions of the articles listed at Entries D69 and D70 and a reprint of the article listed at Entry D73. The fourth essay is a basic introduction to the structure and function of the American Constitution. The book collects papers and lectures that Corwin prepared in conjunction with his visiting professorship at Yenching University in Peking during the autumn and early winter of 1928-1929. See Entries G29-G32.

A9   The Twilight of the Supreme Court: A History of Our Constitutional Theory. New Haven: Yale University Press, 1934.

Reprint: Hamden, Conn.: Archon Books, 1970.

Examines the diminishing role of the Supreme Court at the outset of the New Deal and the resulting effect on the president's and Congress's powers. Corwin's analysis is historical, and he argues for constitutional interpretations that keep pace with modern needs. See Entries G51-G52 and G54.

A10   The Commerce Power Versus States Rights: "Back
           to the Constitution". Princeton: Princeton
           University Press, 1936.

           Reprints: Gloucester, Mass.: Peter Smith,
                      1959 and 1962.

     Analyzes the powers of the federal government over
interstate commerce and criticizes narrow interpretations
of that power in certain New Deal judicial decisions.
Corwin argues that the framers of the Constitution intended to give Congress broad jurisdiction over interstate commerce, but that jurisdiction had been wrongly
curtailed since the late nineteenth century. See Entry
G70.

A11   Court Over Constitution: A Study of Judicial
           Review as an Instrument of Popular Government.
           Princeton: Princeton University Press, 1938.

           Reprints: New York: Peter Smith, 1950; and
                      Gloucester, Mass.: Peter Smith,
                      1957.

     Describes the relationship between the Supreme Court
and Congress in the context of the New Deal. Corwin
examines the effects of judicial review and the need
for the Court to adapt to modern demands. See Entry
G113.

A12.1   The President: Office and Powers. New York:
           New York University Press, 1940.

     A12.2   2nd ed. New York: New York University
                Press, 1941.

     A12.3   3rd ed. New York: New York University
                Press, 1948.

     A12.4   4th ed. New York: New York University
                Press, 1957.

     Reviews the presidency throughout American history
in terms of the office's constitutional origins, purposes, and powers. The book establishes an "institutional" model of the presidency isolating the president's
functions: administrative chief, chief executive, organ
of foreign relations, commander-in-chief, and legislative
leader. Thorough footnotes support the text. See
Entries D148, G122, G127-G130, G148, and G199.

A13.1   Constitutional Revolution, Ltd.   Claremont,
         Calif.:   Claremont Colleges, 1941.

         Reprint: Westport, Conn.:   Greenwood Press,
                     1977.

    A13.2   2nd ed.   Claremont, Calif.:   Claremont
             Colleges, 1946.

Reviews briefly the development of constitutional
theory, especially during the New Deal. Corwin concludes
that constitutional theory has become subject to increased political influence, and that the Supreme Court is
producing results rather than adhering to strict constitutional theory. See Entry G125.

A14   The Constitution and World Organization.   Prin-
       ceton: Princeton University Press, 1944.

       Reprint: Freeport, N.Y.:   Books for Libraries
                   Press, 1970.

Examines the constitutional aspects of participation
by the United States in international organizations and
concludes that there are no constitutional obstacles
to pursuing international peace. See Entry C19.

A15   Total War and the Constitution.   New York:
       Alfred A. Knopf, 1947.

       Reprint: Freeport, N.Y.:   Books for Libraries
                   Press, 1970.

Describes the growth of presidential power and the
erosion of a constitutional balance of powers before,
during, and after World War Two. Corwin determines that
the war permanently altered the structure of government
by expanding federal powers and shifting those powers
among the branches. See Entries E40 and G137.

A16   Liberty Against Government: The Rise, Flower-
       ing and Decline of a Famous Juridical Concept.
       Baton Rouge: Louisiana State University Press,
       1948.

       Reprint: Westport, Conn.:   Greenwood Press,
                   1978.

Analyzes the development of the "liberty" concept from its ancient origins through its place in American constitutional history. Corwin generally praises the expansion of "due process" for the protection of individual liberties. Appendix 1 (at pages 184-188) reprints the book review listed at Entry F123. See Entry G154.

A17.1   Understanding the Constitution. New York: William Sloane Associates, 1949.

    A17.2   2nd ed. Hinsdale, Ill.: Dryden Press, 1958.

Written by Corwin and Jack W. Peltason.

Reviews briefly each clause of the Constitution and describes its meaning and effect. The book is structured much like the book listed at Entry A6, but it lacks that book's breadth of analysis and detailed case citations. Peltason has prepared editions published in 1964, 1967, 1970, 1973, 1976, 1979, and 1982.

A18   A Constitution of Powers in a Secular State. Charlottesville: The Michie Company, 1951.

Collects four essays, including revisions of the articles listed at Entries D153 and D157. Other essays examine presidential powers in foreign affairs regarding nuclear weapons and the "Problem of the Presidency." The nuclear weapons essay reviews the restructuring of American defense in the late 1940s and the inevitable increase in presidential power to defend adequately against nuclear risks. The presidency essay isolates problems stemming from the president's autonomy and dominance within the constitutional framework.

A19   The "Higher Law" Background of American Constitutional Law. Ithaca: Great Seal Books/ Cornell University Press, 1955.

Reprinted from the articles listed at Entries D71 and D72.

A20   The Presidency Today. New York: New York University Press, 1956.

Written by Corwin and Louis W. Koenig.

Analyzes the functions, powers, and elections of presidents in light of the belief that "crisis, and especially international crisis, has become a constant factor of national existence, and that reliance on intermittent recourse to presidential dictatorship is no longer the safe answer." Chapter 2 is revised from the article listed at Entry D170. See Entry G185.

A21   American Constitutional History: Essays by Edward S. Corwin. Edited by Alpheus T. Mason and Gerald Garvey. New York: Harper & Row, Publishers, 1964.

           Reprints: Gloucester, Mass.: Peter Smith, 1970 and 1974.

Collects reprints of the articles listed at Entries D6 (at pages 67-98), D9 and D10 (at pages 46-66), D14 (at pages 25-45), D62 (at pages 1-24), D63 (at pages 99-108), D77 (at pages 109-125), D99 (at pages 126-133), D123 (at pages 134-139), D133 (at pages 140-144), D153 (at pages 197-215), D157 (at pages 145-164), and D162 (at pages 165-196). Most of the reprints are heavily edited. See Entry G207.

A22   Presidential Power and the Constitution: Essays by Edward S. Corwin. Edited by Richard Loss. Ithaca: Cornell University Press, 1976.

Collects reprints of the articles listed at Entries C23 (at pages 1-22), D27 (at pages 23-27), D33 (at pages 28-31), D87 (at pages 55-63), D119 (at pages 63-71), D130 (at pages 72-112), D138 (at pages 112-120), D145 (at pages 141-157), D150 (at pages 157-176), D159 (at pages 137-140), D165 (at pages 121-137), and D181 (at pages 32-53). See Entry G216.

A23   Corwin on the Constitution. Vol. 1, The Foundations of American Constitutional and Political Thought, the Powers of Congress, and the President's Power of Removal. Edited by Richard Loss. Ithaca: Cornell University Press, 1981.

Collects reprints of the articles listed at Entries C22 (at pages 180-194), D16 (at pages 233-239), D34 (at pages 47-55), D35 (at pages 240-245), D51 (at pages 246-271), D62 (at pages 56-78), D71 and D72 (at pages 79-139), D73 (at pages 140-156), D76 (at pages 272-289), D82 (at pages 290-314), D102 (at pages 168-179), D156 (at pages 195-212), and D163 (at pages 213-230). The book also includes a reprint of the book listed at Entry A7 (at pages 317-371) and of the fourth essay in the book listed at Entry A8 (at pages 157-167). See Entries G221-G222. Two additional volumes of this work are planned, but their publication is uncertain.

B
Books Edited by Corwin

B1.1   Otte, E. C. <u>Norway, Sweden and Denmark</u>. Polar Research, by G. T. Surface. The History of Nations, vol. 16. De Luxe Edition. Philadelphia: J. D. Morris and Company, 1907.

    B1.2   De Luxe Edition. Chicago: The H. W. Snow and Son Company, 1910.

    B1.3   University Edition. New York: P. F. Collier & Son, 1913.

    B1.4   Ghent Edition. New York: P. F. Collier & Son, 1916.

    B1.5   Ghent Edition. New York: P. F. Collier & Son, 1920.

    B1.6   Memorial Edition. New York: P. F. Collier & Son Company, 1928.

Presents a general history of the Scandinavian countries from ancient times to the twentieth century. Henry Cabot Lodge was the editor-in-chief of the series.

B2   U.S. Committee on Public Information. <u>War Cyclopedia: A Handbook for Ready Reference on the Great War</u>. Washington: Government Printing Office, 1918.

Edited by Corwin, Frederic L. Paxson, and Samuel B. Harding. Presents elaborate definitions of terminology and concepts related to World War One. See Entry G38.

B3   American Political Science Series. Henry Holt
            and Company, beginning in 1924.

Includes the following books in a series of which
Corwin was the general editor. New books were issued
in the series following Corwin's term as editor, and
editions of Sabine's book have appeared long after
Corwin's tenure. Such subsequent additions are not
listed here.

William Anderson, American City Government. (1925).

William Anderson, American Government. (1938; rev.
      ed. 1942; 3rd ed. 1946).

William Anderson, Fundamentals of American Govern-
      ment. (1940).

Harold H. Bruce, American Parties and Politics.
      (1927; rev. ed. 1932; 3rd ed. 1936).

Raymond Leslie Buell, International Relations.
      (1925; rev. ed. 1929).

Finla Goff Crawford, State Government. (1931).

Henry J. Ford, Representative Government. (1924).

Malbone W. Graham, Jr., New Governments of Central
      Europe. (1924).

Malbone W. Graham, Jr., New Governments of Eastern
      Europe. (1927).

George H. Sabine, A History of Political Theory.
      (1937; rev. ed. 1950).

Henry Russell Spencer, Government and Politics
      Abroad. (1936).

Ellery C. Stowell, International Law. (1931).

B4   U.S. Congress. Senate. The Constitution of
            the United States of America: Analysis and
            Interpretation. 82nd Cong., 2nd sess., 1953.
            S. Doc. 170.

Reviews in detail the historical development and contemporary meaning of each clause of the Constitution. The book is expanded from editions published in 1913, 1923, 1924, and 1938. Later editions also appeared in 1964 and 1973 with supplements in certain other years. Corwin did not contribute to any of the other editions or to the supplements, although the later editions are based on Corwin's work and include his introduction. See Entries C25, D169, G164, and G171.

C
Parts of Books Written by Corwin

C1   Wilson, Woodrow. <u>Division and Reunion, 1829-1909</u>. Epochs of American History. New York: Longmans, Green, and Co., 1909.

Presents a general history of the United States beginning with the election of Andrew Jackson. Wilson wrote the first edition in 1893 and prepared several revised editions. Corwin added chapters to this edition covering the period 1876 to 1909. For Corwin's explanation of his additions and his dealings with Wilson, see the book listed at Entry C21 (at pages 24-26). See Entry C5.

C2   <u>Cyclopedia of American Government</u>. Edited by Andrew C. McLaughlin and Albert Bushnell Hart. New York: D. Appleton and Company, 1914.

       <u>Reprints</u>: New York: Peter Smith, 1930 and 1949; and
                    Gloucester, Mass.: Peter Smith, 1963.

Includes the following essays by Corwin:

"Dred Scott Case," vol. 1, p. 612.

       Describes briefly the content and significance of this 1857 Supreme Court decision.

"Due Process of Law," vol. 1, pp. 614-616.

       Explains the origins of "due process" and its role in American constitutional law.

"Fourteenth Amendment," vol. 2, pp. 40-41.

> Reviews the history, effect, and interpretations of the Fourteenth Amendment.

"Internal Improvement, Constitutional Status of," vol. 2, p. 202.

> Analyzes Congress's power to construct internal improvements such as roads and railroads.

"Trevett vs. Weeden," vol. 3, p. 572.

> Describes briefly the content of this 1786 Rhode Island case, influential in establishing judicial review as a constitutional theory.

C3   "Some Possibilities in the Way of Treaty-Making." In Report of the Twentieth Annual Lake Mohonk Conference on International Arbitration, pp. 65-70. Edited by H. C. Phillips. Lake Mohonk, New York: Lake Mohonk Conference on International Arbitration, 1914.

Analyzes the supremacy of federal law over conflicting state law, thus demonstrating the federal government's ability to enter treaties regulating social and economic policy ordinarily regulated at the state level. Corwin argues for such treaties to enable the United States to keep abreast of world economic policy.

C4   "International Law Imperilled." In The World Peril: America's Interest in the War, pp. 53-81. Written by Members of the Faculty of Princeton University. Princeton: Princeton University Press, 1917.

Examines the violations of international law resulting from the capture of foreign ships and Great Britain's embargo upon all shipments to Germany. Corwin concludes that while the United States entered World War One in self-interest, it must fight to preserve the world's law and order.

C5   Wilson, Woodrow. Division and Reunion. Epochs of American History. New York: Longmans, Green, and Co., 1921.

A more recent version of the book listed at Entry C1. Corwin's additions cover the period through 1918.

C6   "John Marshall and the Constitution." Part 2 of The Age of Jefferson and Marshall. Benjamin Franklin Edition. Chronicles of America Series, vol. 9. New Haven: Yale University Press, 1921.

A separate edition of the book listed at Entry A5.1.

C7   Dictionary of American Biography. Edited by Allen Johnson and Dumas Malone. New York: Charles Scribner's Sons, 1929-1933.

Includes the following brief biographies by Corwin:

"Bradley, Joseph P.," vol. 2, pp. 571-573 (1929).

"Chase, Samuel," vol. 4, pp. 34-37 (1930).

"Field, Stephen Johnson," vol. 6, pp. 372-376 (1931).

"Ford, Henry Jones," vol. 6, pp. 515-516 (1931).

"Marshall, John," vol. 12, pp. 315-325 (1933).

C8   Encyclopedia of the Social Sciences. New York: The Macmillan Company, 1932-1933.

Includes the following essays by Corwin:

"Judicial Review," vol. 8, pp. 457-464 (1932).

        Explains the general purposes, operation, and origins of judicial review in the United States and in other countries.

"Marshall, John," vol. 10, pp. 157-158 (1933).

        Presents a brief biography of Chief Justice Marshall emphasizing his accomplishments in the development of constitutional law.

C9   "Curbing the Court." In The Constitution in the 20th Century, pp. 1-11. Philadelphia: American Academy of Political and Social Science, 1936.

Reprints the article listed at Entry D99.

C10   "The Constitution as Instrument and as Symbol."
           In Authority and the Individual, pp. 191-209.
           Harvard Tercentenary Publications. Cambridge:
           Harvard University Press, 1937.

Reprints the article listed at Entry D102.

C11   "The Schecter Case--Landmark, or What?" In
           Law: A Century of Progess: 1835-1935, vol.
           2, pp. 32-80. New York: New York University
           Press, 1937.

Reprints the article listed at Entry D96.

C12   Association of American Law Schools. Selected
           Essays on Constitutional Law. Chicago: The
           Foundation Press, Inc., 1938.

Reprints the articles listed at Entries D9 and D10
(at volume 1, pages 203-235), D12 (at volume 3, pages
1171-1187), D14 (at volume 1, pages 101-128), D42 (at
volume 2, pages 1060-1068), D51 (at volume 3, pages 565-
593), D55 (at volume 5, pages 514-534), D66 (at volume
1, pages 449-474), D71 and D72 (at volume 1, pages 1-67),
D74 and D75 (at volume 2, pages 1398-1433), D77 (at
volume 2, pages 131-153), D80 (at volume 3, pages 1414-
1433), D82 (at volume 3, pages 103-129), and D120 (at
volume 3, pages 1467-1518). The set of volumes also
reprints the book listed at Entry A7 (at volume 4, pages
1467-1518) and Chapter 1 of the book listed at Entry
A2 (at volume 1, pages 128-173).

C13   "Standpoint in Constitutional Law." In The
           Bacon Lectures on the Constitution of the
           United States Given at Boston University, 1928-
           1938, pp. 407-429. Worcester, Mass.: The
           Heffernan Press, 1939.

Reprints the article listed at Entry D125.

C14   "Report of the Committee on Publications."
           In American Philosophical Society Year Book,
           1938, pp. 82-118. Philadelphia: American
           Philosophical Society, 1939.

Includes at pages 106-107 Corwin's contribution to
the report. Corwin urged publication of a "Library of
American Political Thought" collecting writings of theo-
reticians from Alexander Hamilton to Woodrow Wilson.

C15   "Liberty and Juridical Restraint." In <u>Freedom: Its Meaning</u>, pp. 84-103. Edited by Ruth Nanda Anshen. New York: Harcourt, Brace and Company, 1940.

Analyzes the role of courts as a means of preventing the government from restricting the liberty of individuals. Corwin traces the jurisprudential growth of liberty concepts, and he notes the withdrawal of the Supreme Court from restricting "Constitutional Liberty."

C16   Foreword to <u>Lawyers and the Constitution: How Laissez Faire Came to the Constitution</u>, by Benjamin R. Twiss. Princeton: Princeton University Press, 1942.

            <u>Reprints</u>: New York: Russell & Russell, Inc., 1962; and
                     Westport, Conn.: Greenwood Press, 1973.

Introduces a book analyzing the role of lawyers as intermediaries between businessmen and courts. The book traces the transformation of capitalistic demands into legal doctrine. Corwin also prepared the book for publication after the author's death in 1941.

C17   "Jesse Siddall Reeves." In <u>American Philosophical Society Year Book, 1942</u>, pp. 367-369. Philadelphia: American Philosophical Society, 1943.

Presents an obituary of Reeves, a professor of political science at the University of Michigan.

C18   "The Fundamental Elements of Constitutional Law in the United States of America." In <u>Proceedings of the Eighth American Scientific Congress</u>, vol. 10, pp. 551-559. Washington: Department of State, 1943.

Examines the growth of constitutional law with emphasis on separation of powers, dual federalism, and due process. Corwin finds a merging of governmental powers leading to a breakdown of the traditional theories. Although he is cautious about the merging and growth of federal powers, he concludes that these phenomena translate into a more popular government with "a policy of social leveling."

C19   "The Senate and the Peace (With a Note on Sovereignty)." In <u>The Second Chance: America and the Peace</u>, pp. 143-176. Edited by John B. Whitton. Princeton: Princeton University Press, 1944.

Examines the role of the Senate in foreign relations and concludes that the Senate's function is sometimes anachronistic and usually too cumbersome to be effective. Corwin argues that the Senate's role in treaty-making is that of consultant. But the Senate instead takes a legislative posture and criticizes or amends treaties after negotiations, thereby rendering treaty procedures impractical. Revised from Chapter 3 of the book listed at Entry A14. See Entry D143.

C20   "Dumbarton Oaks and the Constitution--An Interview." In <u>Money and the Law: Proceedings, The Institute on Money and the Law 1945</u>, pp. 131-143. New York: New York University School of Law, 1945.

Analyzes the constitutional issues related to American participation in the proposed United Nations. Corwin writes as if interviewed by a fictitious "Mr. X," highlighting Corwin's theories on delegation of powers, war-making authority, and the practical effects of having a United Nations organization with a strong Security Council.

C21   "Departmental Colleague." In <u>Woodrow Wilson: Some Princeton Memories</u>, pp. 19-35. Edited by William Starr Myers. Princeton: Princeton University Press, 1946.

Captures Corwin's early meetings with Wilson, their shared teaching duties, and Corwin's relations with and reactions to Wilson as president of the United States. Corwin's essay begins in 1905 when Corwin met Wilson while interviewing for a preceptor position at Princeton. It describes the challenges faced while revising Wilson's <u>Division and Reunion</u> (see Entries C1 and C5) and his opinions of Wilson's political career and philosophies.

C22   "The Impact of the Idea of Evolution on the American Political and Constitutional Tradition." In <u>Evolutionary Thought in America</u>, pp. 182-199. Edited by Stow Persons. New Haven: Yale University Press, 1950.

Reprints: New York: George Braziller, Inc., 1956; and Entry A23.

Examines the effects of Spencer's and Darwin's theories of evolution, as well as modern "pragmatism," on American political and constitutional concepts. Corwin finds these conflicting theories leading at times to laissez-faire attitudes and at other times to social activism.

C23   "The Natural Law and Constitutional Law." In Natural Law Institute Proceedings, 1949, vol. 3, pp. 45-81. Notre Dame: College of Law, University of Notre Dame, 1950.

Reprints the article listed at Entry D156. See Entry G150.

C24   "Marshall, John." In The New Century Cyclopedia of Names, vol. 2, p. 2636. Edited by Clarence L. Barnhart. New York: Appleton-Century-Crofts, Inc., 1954.

Presents a brief, general biography of Chief Justice Marshall with emphasis on his contributions to constitutional law. Corwin's credit for writing this entry appears at page xx of volume 1 of the Cyclopedia.

C25   "Legal Status." In Self-Incrimination: A Compilation of the original Dicta published by the Virginia Law Weekly, 1953-54, edited by Lloyd A. B. Mitchell, pp. 19-22. Charlottesville: University of Virginia Department of Law, 1954.

Reprints the article listed at Entry D169.

C26   Essays in Constitutional Law. Edited by Robert G. McCloskey. New York: Alfred A. Knopf, 1957.

Reprints the articles listed at Entries D157 (at pages 185-210) and D165 (at pages 257-274).

C27   "The Office of the President." In Our Presidents and Their Times, p. 3. Columbus, Ohio: American Education Publications, 1958.

Introduces readers to the nature and history of the presidency. Corwin briefly reviews the sources of presidential power and the course of its development through the nation's history. Finally, he summarizes contemporary factors shaping presidential power.

C28   The Natural Law Reader. Edited by Brendan F. Brown. Docket Series, vol. 13. New York: Oceana Publications, 1960.

Reprints excerpts from Corwin's essays listed at Entries C23 (at page 110) and D71 (at pages 111-112). The book collects writings by many scholars to show the development and diversity of natural law theories.

C29.1   "The Aggrandizement of Presidential Power." In The Power of the Presidency. Edited by Robert S. Hirschfield. New York: Atherton Press, 1968.

   C29.2   2nd ed. Chicago: Aldine Publishing Company, 1973.

   C29.3   3rd ed. New York: Aldine Publishing Company, 1982.

Reprints the article listed at Entry D137 (at pages 214-227 of the first edition, pages 245-258 of the second edition, and pages 282-295 of the third edition).

C30   Congress and the Courts: A Legislative History, 1787-1977, vol. 2, pp. 2467-2528. Compiled by Bernard D. Reams and Charles R. Haworth. Buffalo: William S. Hein & Company, 1978.

Reprints the transcript listed at Entry D123.

D
Articles Written by Corwin

D1   "Democracy and Sophistry." <u>Inlander</u> 10 (January 1900): 64-68.

    Studies the relation between democratic principles and sophistry--defined as the practice or teaching of a "captious style or disputation." Corwin cautions that democracy allows artful personalities to gain elected offices, and that the public must not confuse the means of acquiring office with the ends of fulfilling the responsibilities. The <u>Inlander</u> was published by students of the University of Michigan.

D2   "Co-Education." <u>Inlander</u> 10 (February 1900): 93-95.

    Comments on the different attitudes of colleges toward the recent admission of women. Corwin contrasts sharp criticism at Johns Hopkins University with the compromise attitude at Wesleyan College in Connecticut. Corwin draws no conclusion, but ponders where the right solution might lie.

D3   "The Sport of Life." <u>Inlander</u> 13 (December 1902): 87-90.

    Draws on aspects of sports to understand qualities of life. Corwin examines two virtues of sports: imperturbability and loyalty. He then relates these notions to Theodore Roosevelt's vigorous presidency and his call for a "strenuous life." Corwin regards Roosevelt as a sportsman because of his dedicated enforcement of the law.

D4   "The Princeton Preceptorial System." Michigan
            Alumnus 12 (March 1906): 269-272.

Describes the preceptorial system of teaching at
Princeton University and the roles of Corwin and Woodrow
Wilson in the system's operation and development.

D5   "The Supreme Court and Unconstitutional Acts
            of Congress." Michigan Law Review 4 (June
            1906): 616-630.

Reviews the origin and development of judicial review. Corwin offers contradictory evidence of the
framers' intent, but he nevertheless concludes that the
judiciary's power to review legislation, and the president's willingness to ignore adverse rulings, are inevitable developments.

D6   "The Supreme Court and the Fourteenth Amend-
            ment." Michigan Law Review 7 (June 1909):
            643-672.

            Reprint: Entry A21.

Reviews the historical meaning and judicial inter-
pretations of the Fourteenth Amendment to the United
States Constitution and its applications to states.
Corwin traces the Supreme Court's construction of the
Amendment from the early conservative approach through
later decisions overruling state legislation.

D7   "The Establishment of Judicial Review" [part
            1]. Michigan Law Review 9 (December 1910):
            102-125.

Traces the origin and evolution of judicial review
in American constitutional law and jurisprudence. Corwin
discerns that the judiciary's power compels the law to
serve individual litigants, rather than the interests
of the state. See Entry D8.

D8   "The Establishment of Judicial Review" [part
            2]. Michigan Law Review 9 (February 1911):
            283-316.

Continues the article listed at Entry D7.

D9   "The Doctrine of Due Process of Law Before
            the Civil War" [part 1]. Harvard Law Review
            24 (March 1911): 366-385.

            Reprints: Entries A21 and C12.

    Analyzes the early development of the "due process"
concept by courts and commentators. See Entry D10.

D10   "The Doctrine of Due Process of Law Before
            the Civil War" [part 2]. Harvard Law Review
            24 (April 1911): 460-479.

            Reprints: Entries A21 and C12.

    Contines the article listed at Entry D9.

D11   "The Dred Scott Decision, In the Light of Con-
            temporary Legal Doctrines." American Histor-
            ical Review 17 (October 1911): 52-69.

            Reprint: Entry A2.

    Criticizes the Supreme Court's pro-slavery decision
and role in the Dred Scott Case. Corwin sees the decision as a "gross abuse of trust" by the Court, and he
concludes that the Court allowed a desired result to
dictate its decision. See Entry G3.

D12   "National Power and State Interposition: 1787-
            1861." Michigan Law Review 10 (May 1912):
            535-551.

            Reprint: Entry C12.

    Analyzes the constitutionality of a state's seces-
sion from the Union. Corwin argues that the Constitution
is a compact among states, and that the notion of "sovereign states" was not shared by the framers of the
Constitution.

D13   "The Pelatiah Webster Myth." Michigan Law
            Review 10 (June 1912): 619-626.

            Reprint: Entry A2.

Criticizes recent literature proposing that Pelatiah Webster had been the most important contributor to the writing of the Constitution. Corwin refutes such ideas by closely examining Webster's writings and the underlying theories of the Constitution.

D14   "The Basic Doctrine of American Constitutional Law." Michigan Law Review 12 (February 1914): 247-276.

           Reprints: Entries A21 and C12.

Reviews the early history of American constitutional law and the development of the Doctrine of Vested Rights, a theory confirming fundamental rights to individuals. Corwin calls the Doctrine "the first great achievement of courts after the establishment of judicial review."

D15   "Marbury v. Madison and the Doctrine of Judicial Review." Michigan Law Review 12 (May 1914): 538-572.

           Reprint: Entry A2.

Analyzes the origins and underlying theories of the legal basis for judicial review and argues that it results from the common law practice of interpretation and the belief that "judges alone really know the law." Corwin predicts that judicial review will change as new social legislation tends not to permit mechanical interpretations.

D16   "The Treaty-Making Power: A Rejoinder." North American Review 199 (June 1914): 893-901.

           Reprint: Entry A23.

Argues that the reserved powers of the states do not restrict the federal government's treaty-making powers. Thus, a treaty provision can conflict with, and effectively displace, a legitimate state law.

D17   "Making Railroad Regulation National." New Republic, February 27, 1915, pp. 94-96.

Comments on the federal government's expanding power to regulate commerce. Corwin advocates national regulation of railroads, and he asserts that national, uniform regulation allows for simplified bureaucratic mechanisms.

D18   "Is the British Embargo Lawful?" New Repub-
           lic, August 14, 1915, pp. 37-38.

Analyzes the legality of Great Britain's embargo upon
neutral commerce with Germany. Corwin finds that the
blockade illegally interferes with neutral commerce.

D19   "The French Objective in the American Revolu-
           tion." American Historical Review 21 (October
           1915): 33-61.

           Reprint: Entry A3.

Concludes that rivalry with Great Britain over sea
and colonial power motivated France to ally itself with
the American colonies during the American Revolution.

D20   "Game Protection and the Constitution." Michi-
           gan Law Review 14 (June 1916): 613-625.

Argues that Congress acted within its constitutional
powers when legislating protection of migratory birds.
Corwin supports such legislation as part of "the great
movement for the conservation of natural resources, for
the conservation of the navigable streams of the country,
of its forests, of its wildlife; for the elimination
of the natural enemies of community prosperity."

D21   "Sea Rights and Sea Power: The British Embar-
           go." North American Review 204 (October 1916):
           515-530.

Analyzes the legal issues involved in Great Britain's
embargo on all trade with Germany. Corwin examines the
conflict which the United States faced in determining
whether to challenge the embargo and pursue neutral trade
rights with Germany or to acquiesce in light of Britain's
naval strength.

D22   "The Extension of Judicial Review in New York:
           1783-1905." Michigan Law Review 15 (February
           1917): 281-313.

Analyzes the growth of judicial review in New York
courts and isolates important causes and effects of that
growth. Corwin concludes that judicial review grew with
popular approval.

D23   "The Right of Retaliation."   Nation, March
           1, 1917, pp. 233-234.

Describes the rights of neutral countries in the event
of invasion by a belligerent power. Corwin concludes
that a belligerent right of retaliation is limited by
and is subordinate to the rights of neutral countries.

D24   "Pacifism Constitutes New National Problem."
           Daily Princetonian, March 27, 1917, pp. 1,
           4.

Rejects concerns that division among Americans will
keep the United States from successfully waging a war.
Corwin dismisses pacifism and hyphenation as critical
issues, and he shows that unity was not essential in
earlier American wars. Finally, the Professor claims
that Americans are morally, philosophically, and physi-
cally better prepared for war than are the citizens of
other countries.

D25   "Social Insurance and Constitutional Limita-
           tions."   Yale Law Journal 26 (April 1917):
           431-443.

Analyzes the police power of states to enact social
legislation, while limited by the need to protect private
rights. Corwin finds that the trend of judicial decisions favors the exercise of police power rather than
strict enforcement of "freedom of contract" and other
principles.

D26   "Conscription Only is Efficient and Reliable."
           Daily Princetonian, April 14, 1917, pp. 1,
           4.

Details arguments in favor of conscription, rather
than relying on a volunteer military. Corwin asserts
that conscription will lead to a more reliable, stronger,
and better organized military. Moreover, Corwin advocates universal obligatory training.

D27   "War, the Constitution Moulder."   New Repub-
           lic, June 9, 1917, pp. 153-155.

Comments on the effect of war on presidential and
congressional powers. Corwin demonstrates concern about
radical changes in governmental powers during the United
States's early involvement in World War One.

D28   "Validity of the Child Labor Act." New Repub-
          lic, September 15, 1917, pp. 186-188.

Argues that Congress acted within its powers to restrict the employment of children in businesses operating
in interstate commerce. Corwin views child labor abuse
as an evil in need of a remedy, and he cites numerous
Supreme Court cases indicating that such regulation is
within the purview of Congress.

D29   "The Freedom of the Seas." North American
          Review 209 (January 1919): 29-42.

Examines concepts of "freedom of the seas" through
history and in the context of the League of Nations.
Corwin suggests that disarmament and revised policies
of naval warfare are necessary to secure freedom. He
argues against the British policy of maintaining a strong
navy to preserve world peace. See Entry G9.

D30   "Freedom of the Seas Discussed by Corwin."
          Daily Princetonian, February 18, 1919, pp.
          1, 4.

Discloses that the League of Nations proposal does
not preserve the "freedom of the seas." Corwin maintains
that freedom of the seas and international peace can
co-exist by allowing Great Britain to continue its naval
superiority and by recasting the rules of naval warfare.

D31   "Freedom of the Seas--A Compromise." Nation,
          March 8, 1919, pp. 365-367.

Examines provisions of the League of Nations Covenant relating to international control of the oceans.
Corwin looks forward to international control, but is
willing to accept substantial control by Great Britain
and other contries, so long as that control follows a
constitution.

D32   "An Examination of the Covenant." Review,
          June 7, 1919, pp. 77-80.

Reviews the Covenant of the League of Nations and
supports its acceptance by the Senate with reservations.
Corwin states that the United States can continue its
prominent international position even after entering
a cooperative world plan. See Entries E17 and G10.

D33   "Wilson and the Senate." Review, July 26, 1919, pp. 228-229.

    Reprint: Entry A22.

    Criticizes Woodrow Wilson and Congress for the Senate's inability to accept the League of Nations and cautions against the Senate's abdication of powers. Corwin attacks President Wilson and compares Wilson's actions to his early writings about presidential power.

D34   "The Worship of the Constitution." Constitutional Review 4 (January 1920):   3-11.

    Reprint: Entry A23.

    Examines early respect for the American Constitution and concludes that the veneration declined during the Civil War when President Lincoln demanded that the Constitution meet modern needs, regardless of its terms. Corwin concludes that the lack of veneration properly compels the Constitution to be functional and to serve as the "People's Law."

D35   "The Power of Congress to Declare Peace." Michigan Law Review 18 (May 1920):   669-675.

    Reprint: Entry A23.

    Supports the movement in Congress to pass a resolution stating that the war with Germany is at an end. Corwin concludes that although no specific constitutional provision gives the authority, Congress can proclaim an end to the war it originally declared.

D36   "One Year of the Review: What Some Notable Persons Say." Review, May 8, 1920, supp. pp. 3-4.

    Corwin praises the Review at page 3 for ascertaining that "Liberalism should know that it still has a reputable cause. . . ."

D37   "The League, the Constitution, and Governor Cox." Weekly Review, August 25, 1920, pp. 165-167.

Criticizes statements of Governor Cox, Democratic presidential nominee, on the League of Nations and illuminates many details of the treaty. Corwin advances his objections to the League and views the Senate reservations as improvements.

D38   "The Permanent Court of International Justice." Weekly Review, September 29, 1920, p. 265.

Describes and praises the proposed Permanent Court of International Justice as part of the League of Nations. Corwin sees the Court as a means for establishing foreign affairs based on law, rather than on the "intermeddling" of governments.

D39   "The President's Defiance of Congress." Weekly Review, October 6, 1920, p. 282.

Criticizes President Wilson's refusal to obey the Jones Act, requiring him to notify foreign governments of the termination of any treaty with them. The article has no by-line, but Corwin included the essay in a contemporary bibliography of recent publications as part of an annual report of the president of Princeton University.

D40   "Mr. McCall on the Senate." Weekly Review, October 6, 1920, pp. 287-288.

Analyzes the power of the Senate relative to the president and the House of Representatives. Corwin sees Senate power shrinking after increases in presidential authority. The Senate's power to ratify treaties, however, remains an important political check on the president.

D41   "Constitutional Law in 1919-1920" [part 1]. American Political Science Review 14 (November 1920): 635-658.

Reviews select Supreme Court cases on taxation, Prohibition, and free speech. See Entry D43.

D42   "Freedom of Speech and the Press Under the First Amendment: A Resume." Yale Law Journal 30 (November 1920): 48-55.

Reprint: Entry C12.

Examines historical origins of the First Amendment and concludes that legislatures and juries should control the freedom of speech and press. Corwin clearly does not espouse a broad and unbending constitutional right of free speech.

D43   "Constitutional Law in 1919-1920" [part 2]. American Political Science Review 15 (February 1921): 52-70.

Reviews recent Supreme Court cases on treaty-making, admiralty, due process, statutory construction, taxation, public utilities, police power, interstate commerce, the Contracts Clause, and full faith and credit. See Entry D41.

D44   "Constitutional Law in 1920-1921" [part 1]. American Political Science Review 16 (February 1922): 22-40

Reviews recent Supreme Court cases on congressional elections, the Federal Farm Loan Act, taxation, free speech, police power, civil rights, constitutional amendment procedures, and judicial powers. See Entry D45.

D45   "Constitutional Law in 1920-1921" [part 2]. American Political Science Review 16 (May 1922): 228-244.

Reviews recent Supreme Court cases on self-incrimination, searches and seizures, due process, the Sixth Amendment, statutory construction, executive power, free speech, interstate commerce, equal protection, the Contracts Clause, and national supremacy. Corwin concludes with a biographical sketch of Chief Justice White who died during the previous term. See Entry D44.

D46   "The Child Labor Decision." New Republic, July 12, 1922, pp. 177-179.

Criticizes the Supreme Court's holding that Congress could not impose a special tax on employers of child labor. The Court ruled that the statute's regulatory effect on child labor outweighs Congress's legitimate power to impose taxes. Corwin sees the Court making an improper review of Congress's purposes for exercising its constitutional powers.

D47 "Constitutional Law in 1921-1922." American Political Science Review 16 (November 1922): 612-639.

Reviews recent Supreme Court cases on taxation, child labor, interstate commerce, government of territories, constitutional amendment procedures, executive power, judicial power, free speech, due process, statutory construction, and national supremacy.

D48 "Tax-Exempt Securities." New Republic, January 31, 1923, pp. 243-245.

Argues that Congress may tax income from state and local bonds without requiring a constitutional amendment. Corwin notes that local authorities may also tax such income, and that Congress can permit local taxation of national bonds. Corwin asserts that the existing tax-exemption for certain securities is not based on constitutional law. See Entry G14.

D49 "Recent Endeavors to Amend Constitution Reviewed by Professor of Jurisprudence." Daily Princetonian, February 21, 1923, p. 4.

Reviews proposed constitutional amendments that would amend the amendment procedures and eliminate the "lame duck" Congress. Corwin supports both measures, particularly efforts to make amendments more closely reflect popular opinion.

D50 "Professor Corwin Concludes Discussion of Proposed Constitutional Amendments." Daily Princetonian, February 27, 1923, p. 4.

Reviews proposed constitutional amendments regarding taxation of income from government bonds and regulation of child labor. Corwin favors taxation of bond income and criticizes the breadth of the child labor amendment. The essay makes passing reference to the Equal Rights Amendment and proposed amendments giving Congress power over marriage and divorce and ending the Supreme Court's review of acts of Congress.

D51 "The Spending Power of Congress--Apropos the Maternity Act." Harvard Law Review 36 (March 1923): 548-582.

Reprints: Entries A23 and C12.

Supports the constitutionality of Congress's power to spend tax funds for the welfare and hygiene of maternity and infancy. Corwin finds such funding to be within Congress's power to provide for the "general welfare."

D52   "The Three-Mile Limit." Forum 70 (September 1923): 1880-1888.

Argues that the United States has the right under international law to enforce the prohibition of alcoholic beverages within a certain distance from American shores. Corwin reviews the historical development of the three-mile limit, and he concludes that American policy should not interfere with legitimate commerce.

D53   "The Monroe Doctrine." North American Review 218 (December 1923): 721-735.

Traces the origins and evolution of the Monroe Doctrine and concludes that it should not be enforced strictly, or it will become a limitation on foreign policy. Corwin argues in support of the doctrine, demonstrating that its purposes are still relevant and that it is flexible to permit modern needs.

D54   "Constitutional Tax Exemption." Congressional Record. 68th Cong., 1st sess., 1924. Vol. 65, pt. 1, p. 694.

Summarizes Corwin's arguments supporting the constitutionality of taxes on income derived from government bonds. Corwin prepared the essay at the request of Senator R. S. Copeland.

D55   "Constitutional Tax Exemption: The Power of Congress to Tax Income from State and Municipal Bonds." National Municipal Review 13 (January 1924): supp. 51-67.

Reprints: Entry C12;
             Congressional Record. 68th Cong., 1st sess., 1924. Vol. 65, pt. 2, pp. 2023-2028; and
             U.S. Congress. Senate. Committee on Finance. Tax-Exempt Securities. 68th Cong., 1st sess., 1924, pp. 1-18.

Argues that Congress has the power, without further constitutional amendments, to tax income from state and municipal bonds. Corwin suggests a reciprocal measure allowing federal taxation of state bond income and state taxation of federal bond income. See Entries G16-G18.

D56   "No Constitutional Tax-Exemption." New York American, January 22, 1924, p. 24.

Summarizes Corwin's arguments that government securities can and should be subject to income taxation. Corwin asserts that Congress could authorize local taxation of federal securities, and that the Sixteenth Amendment permits federal taxation of state and municipal securities.

D57   "Constitutional Law in 1922-1923." American Political Science Review 18 (February 1924): 49-78.

Reviews recent Supreme Court cases on congressional spending power, interstate commerce, the District of Columbia, Prohibition, judicial power, eminent domain, searches and seizures, statutory construction, due process, the Contracts Clause, ex post facto, and national supremacy.

D58   "Reports of the National Conference on the Science of Politics: Public Law." American Political Science Review 18 (February 1924): 148-154.

Offers a method for objectively analyzing the Supreme Court's judicial review of legislation. Corwin prepared this outline of analytic method in connection with the Conference meeting in Madison, Wisconsin.

D59   "The Presidency." Princeton Alumni Weekly, October 22, 1924, pp. 80-83.

Examines aspects of the presidency, including the president's election, cabinet, and treaty powers.

D60   "The Power of the Supreme Court Over Legislation." New York Law Journal, January 21, 1925, pp. 1505-1506.

Reprint: Entry D61.

Reviews the historical development of judicial review and endorses its survival, despite recent expansions of scope. See Entry G20.

D61   "The Power of the Supreme Court Over Legislation." Chicago Legal News, February 5, 1925, pp. 228, 230-231.

Reprints the article listed at Entry D60.

D62   "The Progress of Constitutional Theory Between the Declaration of Independence and the Meeting of the Philadelphia Convention." American Historical Review 30 (April 1925): 511-536.

Reprints: Entries A21 and A23.

Examines the early development of American constitutional theories, including the separation of powers, judicial review, establishment of individual rights, and the federal treaty-making power. Corwin examines the development in state court cases, in writings by Madison and others, and in theories about the function of the Articles of Confederation.

D63   "Constitution v. Constitutional Theory: The Question of the States v. the Nation." American Political Science Review 19 (May 1925): 290-304.

Reprint: Entry A21.

Reviews the relationship between constitutional theory, as developed by the framers, and constitutional law, as developed by the courts. Corwin concludes that the law should not be burdened by the framers' theories. He regards the Constitution as "a living statute, palpitating with the purpose of the hour. . . ." See Entries G21 and G219.

D64   "Henry Jones Ford." American Political Science Review 19 (November 1925): 813-816.

Presents an obituary of Ford, a former professor of politics at Princeton University and a former president of the American Political Science Association.

D65 "Corwin, Gauss, and Van Dyke Give Views on Court, Advising American Adherence." <u>Daily Princetonian</u>, November 25, 1925, World Court Supp., pp. 3-4.

Advocates that American foreign policy should preserve peace by adhering to the Permanent Court of International Justice. Corwin writes that the United States should seek "a general codification of the international law of peace" and a judicial forum for resolving disputes in international law.

D66 "Judicial Review in Action." <u>University of Pennsylvania Law Review</u> 74 (May 1926): 639-671.

 Reprint: Entry C12.

Analyzes the general nature of judicial review and its applications to American constitutional law. Corwin concludes that courts regard their decisions as final rules of law, decisive "as to <u>cases</u> but also as to questions." Thus, he finds judicial review operating as a conservative influence, protecting existing rights, rather than allowing the law to meet modern needs.

D67 "'Scholarship and Politics Blend in Wilson's Presidency'." <u>Daily Princetonian</u>, February 22, 1927, pp. 4, 9.

Illustrates Woodrow Wilson's political growth through his scholarly pursuits. Corwin reviews Wilson's early writings and academic career as his training for politics. Corwin reveals the sources of Wilson's inspirations and the relationship between those inspirations and his political successes.

D68 "Tenure of Office and the Removal Power Under the Constitution." <u>Columbia Law Review</u> 27 (April 1927): 353-399.

 Reprint: Entry A7.

Analyzes the president's power to remove officials from office and criticizes the extent of that power permitted by the Supreme Court. The Court held that exercise of the removal power could not be subject to Senate approval. Corwin argues that the president should have full power to remove political officers, but administrative officials should be subject to Senate review.

D69   "Some Observations on the Organic Law." China
             Tomorrow, December 20, 1928, pp. 17-20.

             Reprint: Entry A8.

    Analyzes the operation of the Organic Law of China
(promulgated in 1928) with frequent reference and
comparison to the United States Constitution. Corwin
prepared this article in conjunction with his visiting
professorship at Yenching University in Peking.

D70   "Extraterritoriality: an American View."
             China Weekly Review, December 22, 1928, pp.
             154-156.

             Reprint: Entry A8.

    Analyzes China's revolutionary transition from an
extraterritoriality system to an autonomous government
and the judiciary's role in the developments. Corwin
emphasizes the need for an independent and impartial
judiciary to make the new governmental system succeed.
He prepared this article in conjunction with his visiting
professorship at Yenching University in Peking.

D71   "The 'Higher Law' Background of American Con-
             stitutional Law" [part 1]. Harvard Law Review
             42 (December 1928): 149-185.

             Reprints: Entries A19, A23, and C12.

    Examines the historical basis of a "higher law"
shaping American constitutional law and providing "certain principles of right and justice which are entitled
to prevail of their own intrinsic excellence. . . ."
Corwin begins with the premise that the Constitution
is revered by many Americans, and he traces that rever-
ence from ancient Greek philosophies through religious
and political principles. He concludes that in the American Constitution, higher law is based on the notion of
a sovereign people secured by recourse to judicial review
to ensure liberties. See Entries D72, G154, and G219.

D72   "The 'Higher Law' Background of American Con-
             stitutional Law" [part 2]. Harvard Law Review
             42 (January 1929): 365-409.

             Reprints: Entries A19, A23, and C12.

    Continues the article listed at Entry D71.

D73   "The Democratic Dogma and the Future of Politi-
        cal Science." American Political Science
        Review 23 (August 1929): 569-592.

        Reprints: Entries A8 and A23.

    Comments on changes in the study of political science
and its move toward becoming a "laboratory science"
affiliated with behaviorism. Corwin reviews the difficulties of making political study a "natural science,"
but he accepts such developments so long as political
science retains its purpose of "criticism and education
regarding the true ends of the state and how best they
may be achieved."

D74   "The Supreme Court's Construction of the Self-
        Incrimination Clause" [part 1]. Michigan Law
        Review 29 (November 1930): 1-27.

        Reprint: Entry C12.

    Examines historical interpretations of the Fourth
and Fifth Amendments and their contemporary role in American criminal law. Corwin argues that the exclusionary
rule, prohibiting use of evidence illegally obtained,
is a departure from the common law and is detrimental
to criminal prosecution. See Entry D75.

D75   "The Supreme Court's Construction of the Self-
        Incrimination Clause" [part 2]. Michigan Law
        Review 29 (December 1930): 191-207.

        Reprint: Entry C12.

Continues the article listed at Entry D74.

D76   "The Anti-Trust Acts and the Constitution."
        Virginia Law Review 18 (February 1932): 355-
        378.

        Reprint: Entry A23.

    Reviews the constitutionality of federal antitrust
laws and analyzes their applicability to labor unions.
Corwin examines developing interpretations of the Sherman
Act from the narrow views of "interstate commerce" in
early cases through applications of the "Rule of Reason."
He also describes the applicability of the act to labor
strikes, concluding that such construction could violate
the workers' Fifth Amendment "liberty" to strike.

D77   "Social Planning Under the Constitution--A Study in Perspectives." American Political Science Review 26 (February 1932): 1-27.

         Reprints: Entries A21 and C12.

Analyzes the scope of the government's constitutional powers to regulate commercial activity for social purposes. Corwin follows the trends of Supreme Court decisions through history and concludes that constitutional amendments are not necessary for such government regulation.

D78   "Martial Law, Yesterday and Today." Political Science Quarterly 47 (March 1932): 95-104.

Traces the development of martial law in English and American history. Corwin resolves that the president is generally given the discretion to invoke martial law to prevent further public disorder during emergencies.

D79   "Professor Corwin Raises Question of Legality Concerning Regulation Against Alien Students." Daily Princetonian, October 10, 1932, pp. 1, 4.

Argues that the Department of Labor acted illegally in requiring aliens entering the United States as students to prove their financial soundness, notwithstanding any intention to seek employment while attending school. Corwin finds that the regulation exceeds the scope of power that Congress delegated to the department.

D80   "The 'Full Faith and Credit' Clause." University of Pennsylvania Law Review 81 (February 1933): 371-389.

         Reprint: Entry C12.

Details the origin and meaning of the Full Faith and Credit Clause in the Constitution as applied to a variety of situations and legal theories. Corwin determines that the clause is one of the least developed constitutional provisions, and that it allows Congress extensive authority for establishing legal rules to be recognized in all states.

D81   "Constitutional Difficulties Brought Forward
         by Proposed Repeal of Prohibition Amendment."
         Daily Princetonian, February 27, 1933, pp. 1,
         4.

Describes some of the methods for calling state conventions to review the proposed repeal of the Eighteenth
Amendment. Although the procedures are not clearly
delineated, Corwin believes that most reasonable and
representative methods would be constitutional.

D82   "Congress's Power to Prohibit Commerce: A
         Crucial Constitutional Issue." Cornell Law
         Quarterly 18 (June 1933): 477-506.

         Reprints: Entries A23 and C12.

Presents a historical account of Congress's constitutional power to prohibit commerce, in addition to "regulating" it. Corwin argues that business has assumed
a national scale, and that "dual federalism" is no longer
feasible. He raises the issue in light of the National
Industrial Recovery Act provisions prohibiting interstate
commerce not complying with presidential regulations.
See Entry D84.

D83   "Since Congress Didn't." State Government
         6 (June 1933): 6.

Argues that Congress could have called the individual
state conventions to review the proposed repeal of the
Eighteenth Amendment to the Constitution. But in the
absence of congressional action, the states should be
constitutionally permitted to establish their own conventions.

D84   "Constitutional Questions in the New Legisla-
         tion: Outline and Summary of Remarks by Edward
         S. Corwin." Princeton University Alumni Lec-
         tures, June 15 and 16, 1933, pp. 14-18.

Summarizes Corwin's lecture in which he argues that
previous Supreme Court cases offer substantial precedent
to uphold the constitutionality of the National Industrial Recovery Act. His emphasis is on Congress's power
to prohibit interstate commerce and to delegate authority
to the president. The foreword to this pamphlet refers
to the article listed at Entry D82 for "a more extended
statement of Professor Corwin's views."

D85   "The Bases of NRA." New York Times, November
             12, 1933, sec. 4, p. 4.

   Supports the constitutionality of NRA and explains
its necessity. Corwin views NRA not as "revolutionary"
but rather as a response to revolutionary circumstances.

D86   "Moratorium Over Minnesota." University of
             Pennsylvania Law Review 82 (February 1934):
             311-316.

   Analyzes the Supreme Court's holding that a Minnesota statute, enacted to meet emergency needs of the
Depression, does not violate the Contracts Clause of
the Constitution. Corwin believes that the Court's
reliance on emergency needs to sustain the statute may
not support permanent acceptance of New Deal legislation.

D87   "Some Probable Repercussions of 'Nira' on Our
             Constitutional System." Annals of the American
             Academy of Political and Social Science 172
             (March 1934): 139-144.

             Reprint: Entry A22.

   Argues that the New Deal is a constitutional revolution, but that the Constitution can accommodate the
necessary changes. Corwin calls for the Constitution
to cease being a "lawyer's document" and to become a
tool for "considered social purpose." See Entries G47-
G49.

D88   "Supreme Court's Decision on Gold Clause Lauded
             by Members of Princeton Faculty." Daily Prince-
             tonian, February 19, 1935, pp. 1, 3.

   Includes Corwin's comments on the constitutional
soundness of the Supreme Court's ruling in the "Gold
Clause Case."

D89   "Supreme Court Shows It Has Adaptability."
             Washington Post, February 24, 1935, sec. 2,
             pp. 7, 10.

   Reviews the historical development of Congress's power
to coin money and to regulate its value. Corwin demonstrates the growth of Congress's power and the reduction
of the Supreme Court's role.

D90   "Decision on Gold Called 'Strained'." New York Times, February 24, 1935, sec. 2, pp. 1, 18.

Reprints the article listed at Entry D89.

D91   "NRA Verdict Weighed By Famous Authority." Washington Post, June 2, 1935, sec. 4, p. 3.

Reviews the recent Supreme Court decisions rendering certain New Deal legislation unconstitutional. Corwin heavily criticizes the policies and constitutional theories espoused by the Court. He finds the rulings unsupported by facts or judicial precedents.

D92   "President, Court and Constitution" [part 1]. Christian Science Monitor, July 3, 1935, p. 18.

Describes a president's duty when reacting to objectionable Supreme Court decisions in light of the Court's rejection of New Deal legislation. Corwin analogizes to Lincoln's view of the Dred Scott decision and Lincoln's belief that Court rulings do not have constitutional force, but are subject to further review and revision. See Entries D93 and D94.

D93   "President, Court and Constitution" [part 2]. Christian Science Monitor, July 5, 1935, p. 18.

Argues that a president may be justified in not adhering strictly to an objectionable Supreme Court interpretation of the Constitution. Corwin reiterates that Court decisions are regularly overturned and thus should not be viewed as binding. See Entries D92 and D94.

D94   "President, Court and Constitution" [part 3]. Christian Science Monitor, July 6, 1935, p. 16.

Attacks the Supreme Court's power to review the constitutionality of statutes as "arbitrary," and Corwin further asserts that the Court is thereby acting more like a legislature than as a court. He also supports President Roosevelt's open criticism of the Court's rejection of New Deal legislation. See Entries D92 and D93.

D95 "Constitutional Aspects of Federal Housing." University of Pennsylvania Law Review 84 (December 1935): 131-156.

Argues that Congress has the spending power and the eminent domain power to acquire property for low-income housing as part of the National Industrial Recovery Act. Corwin also asserts that Congress may delegate related powers to the president, and that such delegation preserves the Constitution without violating it.

D96 "The Schecter Case--Landmark, or What?" New York University Law Quarterly Review 13 (January 1936): 151-190.

Reprint: Entry C11.

Criticizes severely the Supreme Court's rejection of New Deal legislation and argues that expanded federal regulation of commerce is constitutional and consistent with the framers' intent. Corwin contends that the Court's reasoning leaves unnecessarily broad powers to the states and may undermine the federal government's effectiveness.

D97 "How Far Should the Power of the Supreme Court Extend?" Philadelphia Record, January 12, 1936, sec. 4, p. 9.

Reprint: Congressional Record. 74th Cong., 2nd sess., 1936. Vol. 80, pt. 1, pp. 796-797.

Responds to the Court's rulings against New Deal legislation by concluding that the president and Congress should not view the decisions as "final" determinations of constitutional law. Corwin rejects some proposals for curbing the Court's power--including efforts to "pack" it--and contends that Congress should put the Court "on the spot" and subject it to popular challenges. See Entry G58.

D98 "Curbing the Court." Vital Speeches, March 9, 1936, pp. 373-374.

Reprint: Entry D100.

Reviews possible responses to the Supreme Court's rejection of New Deal legislation and concludes that Congress should not be bound by unfavorable constitutional interpretations. Thus, Congress should freely enact legislation subject to constitutional challenges.

D99   "Curbing the Court." Annals of the American Academy of Political and Social Science 185 (May 1936): 45-55.

Reprints: Entries A21 and C9.

Outlines methods by which the Supreme Court's power over legislation can be restricted. Corwin delivered this paper as part of a radio address series called "The Constitution in the 20th Century." This article is not the same as those articles of identical title listed at Entries D98 and D100. See Entry G64.

D100   "Curbing the Court." American Labor Legislation Review 26 (June 1936): 85-88.

Reprints the article listed at Entry D98.

D101   "How They Are Voting." New Republic, September 30, 1936, pp. 223-224.

Offers, at page 224, Corwin's reasons for voting for Franklin Roosevelt in the 1936 election. Corwin supports the "humanity," "social justice," and "economic stability" of the president's policies, especially the trend toward wider distribution of income.

D102   "The Constitution as Instrument and as Symbol." American Political Science Review 30 (December 1936): 1071-1085.

Reprints: Entries A23 and C10.

Analyzes the Constitution's dual role and argues that the Supreme Court's rejection of New Deal legislation undermines the Constitution's purpose as an instrument of the people's government. Thus, the Constitution's symbolic purposes conflict with its instrumental purposes. See Entries G67-G68, G72-G78, and G82-G83.

D103   "Reform by Amendment Slow and Undemocratic:
            That Method Pushed by Those Who Would Fight
            Changes Hardest--5 Percent of Population Holds
            Veto." Philadelphia Record, November 30, 1936,
            pp. 1-2.

            Reprints: Entries D108 and D115.

    Argues that the process of amending the Constitution
is too uncertain and time-consuming to remedy the Supreme
Court's rejection of New Deal legislation. He also notes
that an amendment is not necessary, because the constitutional clauses in question are open for alternative
interpretations by the Court. See Entries D103-D113
and D115-D117.

D104   "Constitution 'As Is' Sustains New Deal: No
            Point to Amendments 'Adding' to Congress' Pow-
            ers While Court Interprets Vague Doctrines."
            Philadelphia Record, December 1, 1936, sec. 1,
            p. D5.

            Reprints: Entries D109 and D115.

    Argues that Supreme Court decisions striking down
New Deal legislation conflict with earlier decisions,
and that liberal constitutional interpretations would
be preferable to specific constitutional amendments.
Corwin points out that amendments would also be subject
to Court interpretations and would not permit the possible breadth and flexibility of existing provisions.
See Entries D103, D105-D113, and D115-D117.

D105   "Theory of 'Finality' Of Rulings Collapses:
            Jefferson, Jackson, Lincoln and First Roosevelt
            Against It--Court Repeatedly Reversed Itself."
            Philadelphia Record, December 2, 1936, sec. 1,
            p. F12.

            Reprints: Entries D110, D113, and D116.

    Examines the historical significance of Supreme Court
interpretations of the Constitution. Corwin asserts
that Court interpretations are not "final," but are subject to future review and revision by the Court. Thus,
such decisions do not carry the binding force of the
Constitution itself. See Entries D103-D105, D106-D113,
and D115-D117.

D106   "4 Chief Proposals To Curtail Power: Court
            Itself Could Supply the Remedy--It Has Slammed
            Door on New Deal, but Not Bolted It."   Phila-
            delphia Record, December 3, 1936, sec. 1,
            p. D19.

            Reprints: Entries D111, D113, and D117.

    Evaluates four possibilities for changing the Supreme
Court's constitutional interpretations: (1) congressional
expansion of the Court's size; (2) restricting the
Court's subject jurisdiction; (3) requiring more than
a majority vote for overturning legislation; and (4)
congressional veto of Court decisions.   Corwin recommends
that the Court simply exercise its authority to overrule
the New Deal holdings.   See Entries D103-D105, D107-D113,
and D115-D117.

D107   "Court Should Make Only Unanimous Veto: But
            More Immediately, All Judges in U.S. Should
            Be Barred From Office at 70 to Clear the At-
            mosphere."   Philadelphia Record, December 4,
            1936, sec. 1, p. D19.

            Reprints: Entries D112, D113, and D117.

    Argues that the Supreme Court should establish its
own requirement that acts of Congress can be held unconstitutional only by unanimous vote, and that Congress
should require the retirement of judges at age seventy.
See Entries D103-D106, D108-D113, and D115-D117.

D108   "Reform by Amendment Slow, Undemocratic."
            New York Post, November 30, 1936, pp. 1, 10.

    Reprints the article listed at Entry D103.

D109   "Constitution As Is Sustains New Deal."   New
            York Post, December 1, 1936, pp. 1, 16.

    Reprints the article listed at Entry D104.

D110   "Theory of 'Finality' Of Rulings Collapses."
            New York Post, December 2, 1936, p. 13.

    Reprints the article listed at Entry D105.

D111   "4 Chief Proposals To Curtail Power."   New
            York Post, December 3, 1936, p. 13.

Reprints the article listed at Entry D106.

D112   "Court Should Make Only Unanimous Veto."   New
            York Post, December 4, 1936, p. 20.

Reprints the article listed at Entry D107.

D113   "The Problem of the Supreme Court."   Nassau
            Lit 95 (December 1936): 9-10, 25-28.

Revised slightly from the articles listed at Entries
D105, D106, and D107.

D114   "Marxism and Fascism."   Newsweek, December
            12, 1936, pp. 2-4.

Presents capsule definitions of marxism, communism,
and fascism to clarify the concepts for readers.

D115   "Reform by Amendments to Constitution Is Called
            Both Slow and Undemocratic: 5 Per Cent Could
            Block Change, View."   Progressive, December
            19, 1936, p. 2.

Reprints the articles listed at Entries D103 and D104.

D116   "Constitutional Powers of High U.S. Court Dis-
            puted: Views of Justices Holmes, Stone Are
            Cited."   Progressive, January 2, 1937, p. 5.

Reprints the article listed at Entry D105.

D117   "Congress, Supreme Court Itself Could Solve
            Constitutional 'New Deal' Issue: Suggests
            Several Judges Might 'Resign'."   Progressive,
            January 16, 1937, p. 7.

Reprints the articles listed at Entries D106 and D107.

D118   "In My Opinion."   Wharton Review of Finance
            and Commerce 10 (January 1937): 11, 17.

Collects opinions by prominent professors in response to the issue of whether a constitutional amendment is necessary to enlarge governmental power to regulate industry. Corwin argues that the Supreme Court could instead give a liberal construction to the existing language of the Constitution.

D119   "President and Court: A Crucial Issue." New York Times Magazine, February 14, 1937, pp. 1-2, 30.

         Reprints: Entry A22; and
                    U.S. Congress. Congressional Record, appendix. 75th Cong., 1st sess., 1937. Vol. 81, pt. 9, pp. 262-264.

Supports Roosevelt's Court-packing proposal and argues that constitutional law can be correctly altered by changes in the make-up and decisions of the Court. See Entry G89.

D120   "National-State Cooperation--Its Present Possibilities." Yale Law Journal 46 (February 1937): 599-623.

         Reprints: Entries C12 and D124.

Analyzes the relationship between the federal and state governments and concludes that much of the cooperation among governments has been voluntary, rather than constitutionally mandated. Thus, Corwin asserts that the Supreme Court can permit Congress to give financial inducements to the states for complying with national regulations and objectives.

D121   "The Question of the Week: Should Congress Approve or Disapprove Plan to Increase Size of Supreme Court?" United States News, February 15, 1937, p. 4.

Collects opinions of prominent persons on the Court-packing issue. Corwin calls the plan "generally desirable."

D122   "The Supreme Court: Prophecy." Campus: America's College and University Newsfeature Magazine, ca. March 1937, pp. 48-49.

Speculates on the consequences of the passage and non-passage of the Court-packing plan. Corwin fears that non-passage would be viewed as an endorsement of Court policies and that "the obstructive power of judicial obscurantism" would be enhanced. On the other hand, Corwin views the proposal's passage as a boost for contemporary and democratic constitutional philosophy. He suggests that a better proposal would be to permit presidents to appoint three new justices during each term. Campus was apparently distributed without cost at colleges and is not catalogued at any library. The article by Corwin is retained in Box 13 of the Corwin Papers, Princeton University.

D123   U.S. Congress. Senate. Committee on the Judiciary. Reorganization of the Federal Judiciary. Hearings before the Committee on the Judiciary on S. 1392, part 2. 75th Cong., 1st sess., 1937.

Reprints: Entries A21 (incomplete) and C30.

Presents Corwin's opinions about the Court-packing issue and his responses to the questions of Senators on the committee. Corwin contends that a system should be adopted to allow frequent appointments to the Court, thereby opening the Constitution to contemporary interpretations. See Entries G90-G99 and G103.

D124   "National-State Cooperation--Its Present Possibilities." American Law School Review 8 (April 1937): 687-704.

Revised slightly from the article listed at Entry D120. See Entries G100-G101.

D125   "Standpoint in Constitutional Law." Boston University Law Review 17 (June 1937): 513-532.

Reprint: Entry C13.

Argues that the Constitution as a document has been absorbed into constitutional law as merely a reference point, and that constitutional law is derived from external theories and ideas. The result is a "government by allowance of the Supreme Court." But Corwin advocates that the Constitution is the "People's Law," so the Court must adjust its interpretations to meet popular needs and demands. See Entry G105.

D126   "The Court Sees a New Light." New Republic,
        August 4, 1937, pp. 354-357.

        Reprint: U.S. Congress. Congressional Record,
                    appendix. 75th Cong., 1st
                    sess., 1937. Vol. 81, pt. 10,
                    pp. 2077-2078.

Comments on Supreme Court decisions upholding the
constitutionality of New Deal legislation in contrast
to earlier rejection of such legislation. The essay
includes a brief evaluation of the effect of the Court-
packing plan.

D127   "What Kind of Judicial Review did the Framers
        Have in Mind?" Pittsburgh Legal Journal,
        January 8, 1938, pp. 4-20, weekly edition.

Examines diverse theories of judicial review and their
historical developments. Corwin discerns phases of the
evolution of judicial review since 1803 by studying its
varying scope and effect. The article may be Corwin's
most insightful examination of judicial review, and he
concludes that it remains a critical component of constitutional order, but that it is subject to the influences
of public opinion. See Entry G110.

D128   "Question of the Week: Was the President Right
        in Removing Dr. Morgan as Chairman of the TVA?"
        United States News, March 28, 1938, p. 12.

Collects opinions of prominent persons on the issue
of Roosevelt's removal of an official from office. Corwin believes that the president has the duty to obtain
information from officers, and when the information is
refused, he then has the authority to remove the person
from his position.

D129   "The Question of the Week: Could League of
        Nations Have Averted Crisis in Europe By In-
        voking Treaty-Revision Clause?" United States
        News, November 10, 1938, p. 4.

Collects opinions of prominent persons on the title
question. Corwin states his belief that the fighting
in Europe resulted from errors of the British and French
governments, and that he does not favor the calling of
a peace conference by the United States to outlaw war
and to ban the sale of munitions.

D130   "The President as Administrative Chief." Jour-
           nal of Politics 1 (February 1939): 17-61.

           Reprint: Entry A22.

Examines the president's administrative powers and
duties, including the power to appoint and remove officers and to control executive agencies.

D131   "The Posthumous Career of James Madison as
           Lawyer." American Bar Association Journal
           25 (October 1939): 821-824.

Offers evidence that James Madison, "father of the
Constitution," was not a practicing lawyer and never
received formal training in law, thus reinforcing the
principle that the Constitution is a layman's document.
See Entry G118.

D132   "U.S. Begins an Experiment: Will the Neutral-
           ity Act Work?" Newsweek, November 6, 1939,
           pp. 24-25.

Collects opinions of distinguished persons on the
title question regarding the recent act of Congress designed to prevent American involvement in the growing
war in Europe. Corwin comments at page 24 that the act's
effects are speculative, but that Congress has dispelled
the "baleful and fatalistic conviction" of the Roosevelt
administration that America must enter the war.

D133   "Statesmanship on the Supreme Court." American
           Scholar 9 (Spring 1940): 159-163.

           Reprint: Entry A21.

Compliments the Supreme Court for its independence
after the New Deal and projects that the Court will become increasingly able to protect greater individual
liberties. Corwin outlines the Court's new posture and
its effects on states' rights, personal liberty, and
constitutional theory.

D134   "E. S. Corwin Comes Out in Support of Willkie
           Because of Third Term and Foreign Relations."
           Daily Princetonian, October 26, 1940, pp. 1,
           3.

Outlines Corwin's reasons for voting for Wendell Willkie for president. Corwin expresses only one point in Willkie's favor: he can gain the trust of business. But Corwin criticizes Roosevelt on several grounds: the two-term tradition, FDR's early unwillingness to admit a desire for a third term, his "haphazard" foreign policy, and his inability to maintain his early effectiveness.

D135 "The Question of the Week: Would Ending of President's Lend-Lease Power By Congressional Resolution Be Constitutional?" United States News, February 28, 1941, pp. 28-29.

Collects the opinions of prominent persons in response to the title question regarding congressional vetoes of Lend-Lease activity. Corwin concludes at page 29 that an act of Congress can be made to terminate upon any given event, including action by Congress.

D136 "The Question of the Week: Are Our Extensive Naval Patrols Likely to Involve Us in the War?" United States News, May 16, 1941, pp. 28-29.

Collects opinions of prominent persons on the title question. Corwin concludes at page 28 that the extent of United States involvement depends on public reaction to any "shooting" by or upon the Navy.

D137 "Some Aspects of the Presidency." Annals of the American Academy of Political and Social Science 218 (November 1941): 122-131.

Reprint: Entry C29.

Reviews the historical growth of presidential power, emphasizing the presidencies of Jefferson, Jackson, Lincoln, Andrew Johnson, and Franklin Roosevelt. To reverse the growth pattern, Corwin proposes a constitutional amendment requiring the cabinet to comprise members of Congress, thereby balancing and coordinating power between the executive and legislative branches. See Entry G208.

D138 "The War and the Constitution: President and Congress." American Political Science Review 37 (February 1943): 18-25.

Reprint: Entry A22.

Appraises the president's growing powers during the war and criticizes the inability of Congress to exercise its powers. Corwin warns that the emergency powers assumed by the president during the war have become the accepted standard of constitutional law.

D139   "The Senate and Foreign Policy." University of Chicago Round Table, April 4, 1943, pp. 1-22.

Contains a dialogue among Corwin, Nathaniel Peffer of Columbia University, and Quincy Wright of the University of Chicago on the Ball Resolution, a Senate resolution urging the president to initiate development of the United Nations. The discussion centers on the role of the Senate and president in the conduct of foreign affairs. Corwin illustrates his statements with historical examples, and he advocates greater involvement by the public and Congress in presidential decision-making.

D140   "Question of the Week: In View of the Elimination of Mussolini, How Long Do You Think the War in Europe Will Last?" United States News, August 20, 1943, pp. 37-38.

Collects responses of prominent persons to the title question. Corwin states at page 37 that Mussolini's defeat indicates progress in the war effort, and he expects most warfare in Europe to cease within six months.

D141   "Age Makes Case for Revision." Princeton Herald, October 29, 1943, pp. 1, 6.

Urges complete revision of the New Jersey Constitution and illustrates its numerous deficiencies.

D142   "Question of the Week: Should Machinery for Enabling Men in Service to Register and Vote for the Offices of President, Vice President and Members of Congress be Created by the Federal Government or by the Individual States?" United States News, February 11, 1944, pp. 37-38.

Collects responses to the title question. Corwin responds at page 37 that the federal government should control voting procedures, that warfront voting can hamper election processes, and that the voters at home are capable of representing the interests of servicemen.

D143   "La Souverainete dans la Constitution et
        l'Organisation du Monde." La Republique Fran-
        caise 1 (July 1944): 8-10.

   Reprints a French translation of the "Note on Sovereignty" originally published in English as part of the
essay listed at Entry C19.

D144   "Out-Haddocking Haddock." University of Penn-
        sylvania Law Review 93 (June 1945): 341-356.

   Comments on a Supreme Court decision setting forth
a narrow construction of the Full Faith and Credit
Clause. Corwin believes that states must recognize
divorce decrees granted by other states, even if the
decrees involve non-residents. He also argues that Congress has the power to mandate such recognition.

D145   "The Dissolving Structure of Our Constitutional
        Law." Washington Law Review 20 (November
        1945): 185-198.

        Reprints: Entries A22, D146, and D147.

   Examines the New Deal's impact on constitutional law
and concludes that the Constitution has been changed
permanently. Basic concepts, such as the separation
of powers and dual federalism, have eroded from changes
brought by increased demands on the federal government.

D146   "The Dissolving Structure Of Our Constitutional
        Law" [part 1]. New Jersey Law Journal, March
        21, 1946, pp. 1, 3, 5.

   Reprints the article listed at Entry D145. See Entry
D147.

D147   "The Dissolving Structure Of Our Constitutional
        Law" [part 2]. New Jersey Law Journal, March
        28, 1946, pp. 1, 3, 5.

   Continues the article listed at Entry D146.

D148   "How Executive Power Has Increased." Congres-
        sional Digest 26 (January 1947): 5-6.

Examines the various forms of delegation of powers by Congress and the Supreme Court's responses down through the New Deal. The article is excerpted from the book listed at Entry A12.1.

D149   "Electing the President." Think 13 (October 1947): 7-8, 43.

Traces the development of the "Electoral College" as a device for selecting presidents. Corwin suggests that the states mandate election of electors by districts, thereby allowing the electoral vote to parallel popular votes for the candidates.

D150   "Our Constitutional Revolution and How to Round it Out." Pennsylvania Bar Association Quarterly 19 (April 1948): 261-284.

            Reprints: Entry A22; and
                        Philadelphia: Brandeis Lawyers Society, 1951.

Criticizes the expanding governmental powers and concludes that the Constitution has changed from a "Constitution of Rights" to a "Constitution of Powers." Corwin traces the president's powers as commander-in-chief and their impact on private rights.

D151   "Wanted: A New Type of Cabinet." New York Times Magazine, October 10, 1948, pp. 14, 62, 64, 66-67.

Advocates in detail the need for the president's cabinet to comprise members of Congress. Corwin bolsters his proposal with examples of historic propositions for making the cabinet more useful. See Entry G145.

D152   "The Supreme Court as National School Board." Thought 23 (December 1948): 665-683.

            Reprints: Entries A18, A21, and D153.

Criticizes severely a Supreme Court decision holding that the teaching of religious studies during optional "released time" in public schools is unconstitutional. See Entries G144 and G146-G147.

D153   "The Supreme Court as National School Board."
          Law and Contemporary Problems 14 (Winter
          1949):   3-22.

          Reprints: Entries A18 and A21.

Revised from the article listed at Entry D152.

D154   "The Presidency in Perspective."   Journal of
          Politics 11 (February 1949):   7-13.

Comments briefly on the expansion of presidential
powers under certain presidents throughout American
history. Corwin concludes that under Franklin Roosevelt
presidential powers became dangerously personalized.
The article is taken largely from the book listed at
Entry A12.3.

D155   "Who Has the Power to Make War?"   New York
          Times Magazine, July 31, 1949, pp. 11, 14-15.

Analyzes the powers of the president and of Congress
to make war in light of the provision in the Atlantic
Pact treaty requiring participating nations to defend
one another. Corwin sees the pact as promoting a balance
of constitutional powers between the two branches of
the federal government. See Entry G149.

D156   "The Debt of American Constitutional Law to
          Natural Law Concepts."   Notre Dame Lawyer 25
          (Winter 1950):   258-284.

          Reprints: Entries A23 and C23.

Analyzes the role of natural law concepts in American constitutional law. Through historical analysis,
Corwin finds that judicial review and other constitutional theories are rooted in natural law, or "common
right and reason."

D157   "The Passing of Dual Federalism."   Virginia
          Law Review 36 (February 1950):   1-24.

          Reprints: Entries A18, A21, and C26.

Traces the growth of federal powers through American
history, particularly during the New Deal and World War
Two. Corwin examines the effects of domestic and international crises on the structure of constitutional law.

D158   "The Constitutional Law of Constitutional Amend-
            ment."   Notre Dame Lawyer 26 (Winter 1951):
            185-213.

Written by Corwin and Mary Louise Ramsey.

Reviews the historical background of procedures for
proposing and ratifying constitutional amendments.   The
authors argue that Congress should make the final step
each time an amendment is fully ratified by proclaiming
the process complete and the amendment part of the Constitution.

D159   "The President's Power."   New Republic, January
            29, 1951, pp. 15-16.

            Reprint: Entry A22.

Analyzes the growth of presidential power in foreign
affairs and criticizes the president's usurpation of
congressional powers.   The focus is principally on the
president's power to deploy armed forces.

D160   "The Mark Clark Appointment."   Catholic Digest
            16 (January 1952):   86-88.

Reprints a condensed version of the letter listed
at Entry E48.

D161   "Representation at the Vatican."   Catholic
            Mind 50 (February 1952):   76-78.

Reprints the letter listed at Entry E48.

D162   "Bowing Out 'Clear and Present Danger'."   Notre
            Dame Lawyer 27 (Spring 1952):   325-359.

            Reprint: Entry A21.

Comments on developments in judicial interpretations
of First Amendment free speech rights.   Corwin follows
the "clear and present danger" test originated in 1919,
and he concludes that the phrase is no longer a function-
al standard of free speech rights.

D163   "James Madison: Layman, Publicist and Exegete." New York University Law Review 27 (April 1952): 277-298.

Reprint: Entry A23.

Clarifies some misperceptions about Madison and analyzes some of Madison's constitutional theories. Corwin contradicts earlier authority that Madison was a lawyer and further shows that Madison's influence on the drafting of the Constitution was not as significant as generally believed.

D164   "The Issue Rests With Congress." Philadelphia Sunday Bulletin, May 4, 1952, sec. 1, p. 29.

Analyzes the historical development of the president's "Executive Power" in light of President Truman's seizure of steel plants. Corwin concludes that the seizure was justifiable based on precedents and the president's implied powers. He suggests, however, that Congress has ultimate control through its control of funds and its power to regulate the control of industries during strikes.

D165   "The Steel Seizure Case: A Judicial Brick Without Straw." Columbia Law Review 53 (January 1953): 53-66.

Reprints: Entries A22 and C26.

Criticizes the Supreme Court's holding in the Steel Seizure Case and analyzes its historical context. The Court held that President Truman did not have the constitutional authority to order his Secretary of Commerce to seize and operate certain steel mills, thereby averting a nationwide strike.

D166   "Judicial Review and The 'Higher Law'." Think 19 (April 1953): 3-5.

Reviews the historical development of judicial review in the United States thereby upholding the supremacy of the Constitution over state law. Although acknowledging the importance of judicial review, Corwin demonstrates the continuing criticism of it. For example, he points to changing interpretations of constitutional law--especially after the New Deal--weakening the Constitution's reliability and strength.

D167   "The President's Treaty Making Power." Think
        19 (July 1953): 5-7, 30.

        Reprint: Congressional Record, appendix.
                    83rd Cong., 1st sess., 1953.
                    Vol. 99, pt. 12, pp. A4933-
                    A4934.

Analyzes key provisions of the Bricker Amendment
restricting treaty-making power. Corwin concludes that
proposed restrictions are unnecessary, and that the suggested limits on executive agreements do not meet modern
needs for the practical operation of presidential authority.

D168   "Should The State Electoral Vote Be Cast In
        Ratio To Its Popular Vote?" Congressional
        Digest 32 (August-September 1953): 211, 213.

Reprinted from the letter listed at Entry E42.

D169   "Corwin Discusses Legal Status of the Privi-
        lege." Virginia Law Weekly, October 15, 1953,
        pp. 1, 4.

        Reprint: Entry C25.

Reprints Corwin's analysis of the Self-Incrimination
Clause as originally published in the book listed at
Entry B4.

D170   "Of Presidential Prerogative." Whittier Col-
        lege Bulletin 47 (September 1954): 3-27.

        Reprint: Entry A20.

Examines the historical growth of presidential powers, with criticism of Franklin Roosevelt's assumption
of new powers before and during World War Two. Corwin
begins with the theory that presidential prerogative
is the product of presidential personality, crisis, and
available constitutional doctrine. He concludes with
a call for restriction on the executive's power.

D171   "Professors, Students Take Part In Panel
        Segregation Conference." Daily Princetonian,
        November 11, 1954, pp. 2-4.

Includes Corwin's statements while participating in a panel discussion of the 1954 Brown v. Board of Education decision. Corwin states that the Supreme Court perhaps went too far in responding to segregation, and that Congress will have to establish a gradual system of school integration.

D172   "John Marshall." Washington: United States Commission for the Celebration in 1955, of the Two Hundredth Anniversary of the Birth of John Marshall, 1955.

Presents a biographical sketch of Marshall and an outline of his significant contributions to constitutional law. The pamphlet was intended as background information for a film-discussion program entitled "Great Men and Great Issues in Our American Heritage."

D173   [Untitled: Obituary of Charles Warren]. American Historical Review 60 (January 1955): 492-493.

Reviews Warren's accomplishments and contributions as a legal historian. Corwin praises Warren's writings, but criticizes some of his theories. The obituary has no by-line; the Corwin Papers at Princeton, however, reveal that Corwin was its author.

D174   "Our Expendable Constitution." University of Illinois Bulletin 52 (January 1955): 3-20.

Analyzes the growth of federal powers, with emphasis on presidential war powers and on the continued power expansion during peace. The essay reviews the growth of presidential powers before and during World War Two, the effect of atomic weapons on foreign policy, and the lasting consequences of certain constitutional decisions by the Supreme Court.

D175   "Case Against Bricker Amendment." New York Herald Tribune, May 23, 1955, p. 14.

Presents Corwin's arguments opposing adoption of the Bricker Amendment, a proposed constitutional amendment limiting the government's authority to make treaties and executive agreements. See Entry G181.

D176   "John Marshall, Revolutionist <u>Malgre Lui</u>."
<u>University of Pennsylvania Law Review</u> 104
(October 1955): 9-22.

Outlines Marshall's background and principal constitutional theories and traces their impact on Supreme Court
decisions through the New Deal. Corwin notes that Marshall's decisions were used to support the constitutionality of New Deal legislation, but he argues that Marshall would not have approved of the revolutionary
changes brought during that era.

D177   "Presidential 'Inability'." <u>National Review</u>,
November 26, 1955, pp. 9-10.

Contains Corwin's answers to questions on constitutional processes in the event of the president's inability to perform his duties. Among his answers, Corwin
suggests that Congress could designate the cabinet or
other body to determine whether the president is able
to serve in office.

D178   U.S. Congress. Senate. Committee on Government Operations. <u>Hearings on Proposal to
Create Position of Administrative Vice Presi-
dent</u>. 84th Cong., 2nd sess., 1956.

Sets forth at page 34 Corwin's letter to the Committee
that an "Administrative Vice President" is not necessary. Corwin believes that the chief of staff and other
White House aides suitably fulfill the needed tasks.

D179   U.S. Congress. House. Committee on the
Judiciary. <u>Presidential Inability</u>. 84th
Cong., 2nd sess., 1956.

Reports at pages 16-17 Corwin's responses to a series
of questions about presidential inability. Corwin provides his opinions on temporary and permanent disability,
the determination of disability, and the vice president's
succession to the higher office.

D180   "Franklin and the Constitution." <u>Proceedings
of the American Philosophical Society</u> 100 (August 31, 1956): 283-288.

Reviews Benjamin Franklin's contributions to the development of constitutional law. Franklin's contributions were few and insubstantial. Corwin's principal purpose is to praise Franklin as the "First American and first American Citizen of the World." See Entry G208.

D181   "Woodrow Wilson and the Presidency." Virginia Law Review 42 (October 1956): 761-783.

Reprint: Entry A22.

Analyzes President Wilson's perspectives on the presidency, including Wilson's early writings on the office. The article moves from Wilson's early years at Princeton through Corwin's conclusions about Wilson's impact on the presidency. See Entries G188-G189.

D182   "How to Become President." Catholic Digest 21 (November 1956): 32-33.

Written by Corwin and Louis W. Koenig.

Examines the vice presidency and the frequency of vice presidents ascending to the presidency. The article is condensed from the book listed at Entry A20 and emphasizes important functions served by the current vice president--Richard Nixon.

D183   "Problem of Presidential Disability." New York Herald Tribune, December 4, 1957, p. 24.

Excerpts from the book listed at Entry A12.4 Corwin's observations on the vice president's succession to the presidency upon the president's death or disability. Corwin reviews historical succession procedures and comments on the contemporary succession order. The Professor believes that the Secretary of State is generally preferable to the Speaker of the House as a successor. Eisenhower's recent stroke made the issue keenly relevant.

D184   "Supreme Court's 'Vicious Nonsense'." Richmond Times-Dispatch, April 3, 1958, p. 12.

Reprints excerpts from the letter listed at Entry E55.

D185   "Fiftieth Anniversary Greetings."   America,
         March 28, 1959, pp. 742-743.

Includes at page 743 Corwin's appraisal of America
upon the magazine's fiftieth anniversary of publication.

E
"Letters to the Editor"
Written by
Corwin

E1   "Roosevelt and the Courts." New York Evening Post, December 11, 1908, p. 6.

Explains that "the decisions of courts upon social questions depend upon their social theories." Thus, Corwin determines that constitutional law, like common law, has public policy as its foundation. Corwin believes that public policy offers "a much securer foundation than that furnished by the conception of precedent as binding. . . ."

E2   "Workingmen's Compensation Law." New York Evening Post, March 30, 1911, p. 8.

Criticizes a New York Court of Appeals ruling that portions of the state workman's compensation laws are unconstitutional. Corwin argues that the law is a needed protection for employees, and that such regulation is not an unconstitutional exercise of state police powers.

E3   "The Income Tax Amendment." New York Evening Post, May 18, 1911, p. 8.

Counters key arguments against adoption of the Sixteenth Amendment authorizing a federal income tax. Corwin demonstrates that the Amendment would not permit a tax on state and municipal bonds themselves, but only on income derived from them. Corwin asserts that the tax should reach all individuals and all wealth, regardless of disparities in wealth concentration among the states.

E4   "'Income Tax Ratification'." New York Evening
          Post, January 25, 1912, p. 8.

   Affirms succinctly Corwin's support for the Sixteenth
Amendment and the need to institute an equitable system
of taxing wealth wherever located.

E5   "National Supremacy." Nation, February 5,
          1914, p. 134.

   Objects to a review of Corwin's book listed at Entry
A1 and asserts the thesis that state laws are subordinate
to national treaty-making power.

E6   "The Alien Labor Law: Prof. Corwin Sees Good
          Reason to Doubt Its Constitutionality." New
          York Times, November 24, 1914, p. 12.

   Argues vehemently that a proposed act prohibiting
employment of aliens on public works projects is unconstitutional. Corwin states that the Equal Protection
Clause guards the rights of aliens to employment.

E7   "For Undefined Preparedness." New Republic,
          December 25, 1915, p. 199.

   Argues that the United States must act to protect
itself from foreign invasion before the country can examine and redefine its foreign policy.

E8   "Concerning Mr. Angell: Professor Corwin
          Agrees With Only One Point." Daily Prince-
          tonian, February 26, 1916, p. 2.

   Criticizes a speech suggesting that the United States
define its foreign policy before implementing preparedness actions. Corwin notes that the country is no longer
protected by geographical isolation, and that it must
be prepared to defend itself before it can formulate
effective policies.

E9   "A 'Firm' Foreign Policy." New York Evening
          Post, October 26, 1916, p. 8.

Evaluates Woodrow Wilson's foreign policy. Although "strongly" favoring the election of Charles Evans Hughes in the 1916 election against Wilson, Corwin dispells much of the usual criticism of Wilson's foreign policies. He demonstrates, however, that the Wilson administration itself often creates the image that its policies are not firm.

E10   "The Status of Interned Ships." New York Evening Post, February 5, 1917, p. 8.

Explains that under international law only German ships in American waters at the time hostilities with Germany begin may be requisitioned and used by the United States until hostilities cease. Moreover, the United States would be permitted to confiscate any German ships intended for conversion into warships.

E11   "Believes Negotiation Unthinkable." New Republic, August 25, 1917, p. 107.

Criticizes sharply negotiations and peace initiatives proposed by Pope Benedict. Corwin believes that the proposal would condone Germany's "outrage upon law and humanity."

E12   "Professor Corwin's Views." New York Evening Post, October 4, 1918, p. 7.

Comments on the authenticity of classified German documents disclosing secret war information.

E13   "Political Reform in Germany." New York Evening Post, November 2, 1918, p. 8.

Responds to a speech by the German Chancellor, Prince Max of Baden, about European political institutions. Corwin criticizes the Chancellor's rhetoric and lack of democratic appeal.

E14   [Untitled.] American Historical Review 24 (January 1919): 306-307.

Criticizes bitterly John Bassett Moore's review of Corwin's book listed at Entry A4. Corwin recites specific statements by Moore and gives counter-arguments.

E15   "Ending the War." New York Times, June 4,
           1919, p. 14.

   Argues that a treaty is not the only means of termi-
nating a war. Congress as a whole can declare the end
of a war, and it rightfully has that power because of
its authority to maintain the armed forces.

E16   "The Great Powers and the Covenant." Review,
           July 5, 1919, p. 167.

   Expands on arguments in support of the League of
Nations and emphasizes the need for nations to settle
disputes together.

E17   "Professor Corwin's Reply." Review, August
           30, 1919, pp. 343-344.

   Responds to the letter listed at Entry G10 and details Corwin's views of the Shantung Agreement of the
Treaty of Versailles. Corwin reinforces his objections
to the League of Nations and emphasizes the League's
detriments over its advantages.

E18   "Congress's Right to Declare Peace." Review,
           April 17, 1920, p. 388.

   Clarifies the constitutional power of Congress to
"make peace" in the absence of a specific clause in the
Constitution permitting such power. Corwin argues that
Congress has the right to repeal previous enactments--
such as its declaration of war--and to compel peace by
prohibiting commerce with countries at war.

E19   "The League and the Court." New York Times,
           September 3, 1920, p. 8.

   Describes the operation and authority of the League
of Nations and the Hague Court. Corwin supports Senator
Warren Harding's observations on the effect of the League
of Nations. See Entry G12.

E20   "League's Shortcomings." New York Times, Sep-
           tember 29, 1920, p. 8.

   Responds to the letter listed at Entry G12 and elaborates on Corwin's views of the League of Nations.

E21   "A Possible Way Out." Weekly Review, December
       22, 1920, pp. 617-618.

Criticizes some actions of the League of Nations and
suggests different methods for its operation. Corwin
shows some optimism about the League and its potential.
With the June 16, 1920 issue, the Review became the Weekly Review.

E22   "Lincoln and Fort Sumter." New York Times,
       June 27, 1922, p. 14.

Explains that President Lincoln sent food and provisions to Fort Sumter when an attack by the South was
threatened. Corwin asserts that Lincoln did not supply
men, arms, or ammunition.

E23   "Liquor in Possession: If Properly Acquired
       Abroad Does the Act Prohibit Its Transporta-
       tion?" New York Times, October 11, 1922, p.
       18.

Criticizes an attorney general opinion concluding
that Prohibition extends to American vessels on the high
seas and to foreign vessels entering American waters.
Corwin believes that the language of the Eighteenth Amendment and subsequent acts of Congress do not allow such
interpretations.

E24   "Changing the Dry Law." New York Times, April
       19, 1926, p. 18.

Analyzes the power of Congress and the states to regulate the sale and transportation of alcoholic beverages
during Prohibition. Corwin argues that the states and
Congress have equal authority, within their respective
jurisdictions, to make such regulations.

E25   "Rebukes Communication of '1928': Corwin Finds
       Senior Errs in Attitude Toward Teaching and
       Research Activities." Daily Princetonian,
       December 12, 1927, p. 2.

Responds to a student's letter attacking the Politics
Department and Princeton University at large for the
lack of emphasis on teaching quality. Corwin vigorously
condemns the charges and defends the need for professors
to supplement teaching with research.

E26   "Legal Bases of Rate Making." New York Times,
           May 25, 1930, sec. 3, p. 10.

Defends the power of governments to regulate utility
rates for providing a fair return on investment and for
protecting the public interest.

E27   "Congress and Power Rates." New York Times,
           June 22, 1930, sec. 3, p. 8.

Elaborates on the government's power to regulate
utility rates. Corwin asserts that electric power and
tangible commodities, once crossing state lines, can
be subject to federal regulation. See Entry G33.

E28   "Controverting Mr. Sundean: Theoretically,
           Repeal Plan Would Work, It Is Contended."
           New York Times, September 4, 1932, sec. 2,
           p. 2.

Describes the procedures and background of amending
the Constitution by means of conventions in states rather
than through state legislatures. Corwin reasons that
Congress has the authority to call state conventions
for pursuing amendments.

E29   "Defends Politics Reading System: Professor
           Corwin Objects to Suggested Segregation of
           Junior Members of the School." Daily Prince-
           tonian, October 10, 1933, p. 2.

Affirms the Politics Department policy not to segre-
gate its students from students in the School of Public
and International Affairs. See Entry G44.

E30   "Forgotten for Cause." New York Times, January
           6, 1934, p. 14.

Explains the historical background and meaning of
a "forgotten" clause of the Fourteenth Amendment regarding the public debt. Corwin emphasizes that the provision refers only to a post-Civil War debt and not to
any subsequent debt.

E31   "The Court Personnel: Application of Sumners-
           M'Carran Act Regarded as a Solution." New
           York Times, May 30, 1937, sec. 4, p. 9.

Explains the effect of a Supreme Court justice's retirement on his status as a "Judge of the United States."

E32   "Madison and the Law: Records Held to Show He Was Not Member of Bar." New York Times, October 17, 1937, sec. 4, p. 8.

Reviews evidence that President James Madison neither studied nor practiced law. Corwin notes with satisfaction that the "clear" language of the Constitution includes neither a "whereas" nor an "aforesaid." See Entry G109.

E33   "Prof. Corwin Replies: Princetonian Defends His Use of the Hughes Quotation." New York Sun, November 29, 1938, p. 20.

Explains that Corwin does not find hostility in Chief Justice Hughes's statement: "We are under a Constitution, but the Constitution is what the judges say it is." Corwin uses the quotation in one of his books to offer insight, not to slur the courts.

E34   "Congressional Power to Withdraw Privilege Denied." New York Times, February 19, 1939, sec. 4, p. 9.

Analyzes the president's power to appoint governmental officials with and without the advice and consent of the Senate. Corwin clarifies that Senate approval is needed for appointments, not nominations, and that approval need not be unanimous. See Entry G114.

E35   "President's Stand Criticized: His Arguments for Repeal of Embargo Are Called Inconclusive." New York Times, October 2, 1939, p. 16.

Criticizes severely President Roosevelt's reasons for repealing the arms embargo, but suggests that many other reasons may be valid and convincing. The letter reflects Corwin's growing objections to Roosevelt, concluding that the repeal "shows a disturbing lack of clarity on the part of the Administration as to its own guiding intentions."

E36   "Executive Authority Held Exceeded in Destroyer
       Deal." New York Times, October 13, 1940,
       sec. 4, pp. 6-7.

   Criticizes at length President Roosevelt's Destroyer-
Bases Agreement and outlines numerous constitutional
and statutory violations. Corwin sees the action as
"an endorsement of unrestrained autocracy in the field
of our foreign relations" and concludes that general
approval of the action "renders the breach of constitutional forms by which it was accomplished at once the
less excusable and the more dangerous as a precedent."
Corwin urges the president at least to submit the agreement for congressional ratification. See Entry G119.

E37   "Professor Corwin 'Repents'." Daily Princeton-
       ian, October 31, 1940, p. 2.

   Presents Corwin's self-repentence for signing a peti-
tion regarding "student behavior at the movies." Corwin
analogizes the situation to criminal investigations of
critics of the Roosevelt administration, and the Professor warns about both incidents: "we had better exercise
our liberties while we still have them."

E38   "Convoys Debated: Court Ruling Held to Place
       Power With Congress." New York Times, February
       23, 1941, sec. 4, p. 9.

   Argues that Congress has the power to prohibit the
president's deployment of naval convoys for protecting
British merchantmen. Corwin bases his theory on Congress's power to declare war and thus to authorize all
acts of hostility. See Entry G126.

E39   "An Opportunity Overlooked: Republican Pledge
       to Two-Thirds Vote On Agreements Is Criti-
       cized." New York Times, June 30, 1944, p. 20.

   Criticizes the Republican platform proposing that
all international agreements be supported by a two-thirds
vote of the Senate. Corwin expresses concern that even
the platform's ideals may not revive Senate strength
in foreign affairs. See Entry G134.

E40   [Untitled.] New York Times Book Review, June
       1, 1947, p. 19.

Responds to Judge Jerome Frank's review of the book listed at Entry A15 and argues that the book's emphasis is not on the New Deal. See Entry G143.

E41   "Intent." New York Times Magazine, August 8, 1949, pp. 2, 4.

Examines the role of sedition and utterances in First Amendment analysis. Corwin argues that the "clear and present danger" test favors free speech with a minimum of restrictions.

E42   "Choosing a President: Shortcomings Seen in Proposal to Reform Electoral System." New York Times, February 5, 1950, sec. 4, p. 8.

        Reprint: Entry D168.

Reviews the operation of the electoral system and proposes some changes. Corwin argues for retention of the basic electoral system, "ridiculous as it is in some respects. . . ."

E43   "Congressional investigations." America, July 7, 1951, p. 367.

Argues that the Supreme Court should restrict the right of Congress to hold televised hearings. Corwin believes that hearings have invaded the privacy of some persons being questioned and have been little more than publicity forums for legislators.

E44   "Edward Corwin Requests By-Pass for Princeton." Princeton Herald, August 1, 1951, p. 4.

Registers Corwin's complaint about truck traffic in front of his house on Stockton Road and the need for a Princeton by-pass. Even in such common circumstances, Corwin takes a constitutional perspective; he cites a Supreme Court case when calling for safety measures restricting traffic.

E45   "Presidential Lawmaking." New York Times, August 19, 1951, sec. 4, p. 8.

Criticizes the president's ability to issue orders on subjects normally appropriate for congressional acts.

E46   "Military Jurisdiction: Precedent for Arrest
           and Trial in Holohan Death Cited." New York
           Times, September 2, 1951, sec. 4, p. 6.

Describes an early precedent for the scope of jurisdiction of military courts. See Entry E47.

E47   "Legislation on Courts-Martial." New York
           Times, September 14, 1951, p. 24.

Emphasizes that the letter listed at Entry E46 argues
only that no constitutional provision restricts the jurisdiction of military courts in the Holohan murder case.

E48   "Vatican Post Discussed: Constitutional As-
           pects of President's Action are Considered."
           New York Times, November 12, 1951, p. 24.

           Reprints: Entries D160 and D161.

Argues that the president's right to recognize governments and to send an ambassador to the Vatican outweighs
any separation of church and state principles. Corwin
notes that political reasons support sending an ambassador, and that there may be no procedure for challenging
the constitutionality of such action. See Entries G156-
G158 and G160.

E49   "Decline of the Executive." New Republic,
           June 15, 1953, p. 2.

Defends Eisenhower's problems during early months
in office as the result of political inexperience which
will change in the near future. Corwin also defends
the two-term limit on the presidency, claiming that Americans were "hood-winked into re-electing into office in
1944 a very sick man. . . ." Corwin lightly criticizes
Eisenhower for appointing "nine millionaires" to his
cabinet.

E50   [Untitled.] American Historical Review 60
           (January 1955): 496-497.

Offers evidence of James Madison's opinion about control of the West by the Eastern states. Madison at one
time likened Virginia's control over the territory of
Kentucky to a "right of the crown." See Entry G177.

E51   "Electing Our Presidents: Proposal to Abolish
            the Electoral College Is Queried." <u>New York
            Times</u>, July 5, 1955, p. 28.

Argues for preserving the electoral system and criticizes Senator Hubert Humphrey's proposed abolition of
it. Corwin makes two principal arguments. First, he
sees popular votes as too difficult to police and to
count for reliability. Second, he argues that a low
popular vote per elector actually results in a better
representation of interests.

E52   "Electoral System Supported: Election of Can-
            didate With Stronger Popular Following Held
            Guaranteed." <u>New York Times</u>, December 26,
            1956, p. 26.

Argues that, in the absence of a strong third party,
the electoral system guarantees that the candidate with
the strongest popular support will be elected. Corwin
asserts that the lower popular vote for the winning candidates in 1876 and 1888 resulted from election fraud.
See Entry G191.

E53   "Presidential Disability." <u>New York Times</u>,
            April 7, 1957, sec. 4, p. 10.

Reasons that the Necessary and Proper Clause of the
Constitution allows Congress to prescribe responses to
presidential disability.

E54   "Taking Fifth Amendment: Supreme Court Version
            of Provision on Self-Incrimination Criticized."
            <u>New York Times</u>, August 15, 1957, p. 20.

Argues that the Self-Incrimination Clause prohibits
forcing a criminal defendant to testify against himself,
but should not allow a witness to refuse to testify before a Senate committee. Corwin attacks the Warren Court
for allowing such interpretations of the Constitution.
See Entry G192.

E55   "Limiting the Judiciary: Remedy Proposed for
            Impingement by Supreme Court on Other Bran-
            ches." <u>New York Times</u>, March 16, 1958, sec. 4,
            p. 10.

            <u>Reprint</u>:   Entry D184.

Argues for a restriction of the Supreme Court's jurisdiction over congressional and executive actions. Corwin attacks the Warren Court for its "weird" rulings that invade legislative prerogatives. See Entries E56, G196-G197, and G209.

E56   "Congress and the Judiciary: Trend in Recent Supreme Court Decisions Questioned." New York Times, April 19, 1958, p. 20.

Elaborates on Corwin's letter listed at Entry E55.

E57   "A Shrine for a Founder." Washington Post, July 12, 1959, sec. E, p. 4.

Supports the proposal for a monument in Washington in honor of James Madison, but Corwin notes that many other prominent Americans also deserve such ceremony.

E58   "Bi-State Compact Queried." New York Times, May 29, 1960, sec. 4, p. 6.

Notes the constitutional requirement that states obtain congressional approval before executing agreements with one another.

F
Book Reviews Written by Corwin

F1   A History of the United States and its People
      from Their Earliest Records to the Present
      Time, vol. 1, by Elroy McKendree Avery. Annals
      of the American Academy of Political and Social
      Science 25 (May 1905): 182-184.

F2   The American Revolution, by Claude Halstead
      Van Tyne. Michigan Alumnus 12 (April 1906):
      311-317.

F3   The Confederation and the Constitution, by
      Andrew Cunningham McLaughlin. Michigan Alum-
      nus 12 (June 1906): 413-422.

F4   A History of the United States and Its People,
      vol. 2, by Elroy McKendree Avery. Annals of
      the American Academy of Political and Social
      Science 28 (November 1906): 113-115.

F5   Slavery and Abolition, 1831-1841, by Albert
      Bushnell Hart; Westward Extension, 1841-1850,
      by George Pierce Garrison; Parties and Slavery
      1850-1859, by Theodore Clarke Smith; and Causes
      of the Civil War 1859-1861, by French Ensor
      Chadwick. American Political Science Review
      2 (November 1907): 110-118.

F6   The Assassination of Abraham Lincoln and its
      Expiation, by David N. DeWitt. American His-
      torical Review 14 (July 1909): 860.

F7   A History of the President's Cabinet, vol.
      1, by Mary L. Hinsdale. Michigan Alumnus 18
      (April 1912): 338.

F8   Social Reform and the Constitution, by Frank
      J. Goodnow. American Political Science Review
      6 (May 1912): 270-276.

F9   Our Judicial Oligarchy, by Gilbert E. Roe.
      American Political Science Review 6 (November
      1912): 654-655.

F10   The Power of the Federal Judiciary Over Legis-
      lation, by J. Hampden Dougherty; and The Su-
      preme Court and the Constitution, by Charles
      A. Beard. American Political Science Review
      7 (May 1913): 329-332.

F11   The Fourteenth Amendment and the States, by
      Charles Wallace Collins. Political Science
      Quarterly 28 (June 1913): 334-336.

F12   History of the Supreme Court of the United
      States, by Gustavus Myers. American Political
      Science Review 7 (August 1913): 500-502.

F13   An Economic Interpretation of the Constitution
      of the United States, by Charles A. Beard.
      History Teacher's Magazine 5 (February 1914):
      65-66.

F14   Notes on the Science of Government and the
      Relations of the States to the United States,
      by Raleigh C. Minor. American Political Sci-
      ence Review 8 (February 1914): 144-145.

F15   The Supreme Court of the United States and
      its Appellate Power under the Constitution,
      by Edwin Countryman. American Political Sci-
      ence Review 8 (August 1914): 503-504.

F16　　　The Judicial Veto, by Horace A. Davis. New Republic, January 23, 1915, pp. 28-29.

F17　　　The Validity of Rate Regulations, State and Federal, by Robert P. Reeder. American Political Science Review 9 (February 1915): 160-163.

F18　　　European Police Systems, by Raymond B. Fosdick. Princeton Alumni Weekly, April 28, 1915, pp. 702-703.

F19　　　Government of the Canal Zone, by George W. Goethals. Princeton Alumni Weekly, October 6, 1915, p. 42.

F20　　　The Diplomatic Protection of Citizens Abroad or the Law of International Claims, by Edwin M. Borchard. New Republic, May 20, 1916, pp. 70-72.

F21　　　The Postal Power of Congress, a Study in Constitutional Expansion, by Lindsay Rogers. American Political Science Review 10 (November 1916): 773-775.

F22　　　Life of John Marshall, vols. 1 and 2, by Albert J. Beveridge. Mississippi Valley Historical Review 4 (June 1917): 116-118.

F23　　　Nationalism and Internationalism, by Ramsey Muir. American Political Science Review 12 (August 1918): 546-547.

F24　　　Miscellaneous Addresses, by Elihu Root. American Historical Review 14 (October 1918): 132-133.

F25　　　Beaumarchais and the War of American Independence, by Elizabeth S. Kite. American Historical Review 14 (January 1919): 293-294.

F26   From Isolation to Leadership: A Review of American Foreign Policy, by John Holladay Latane. American Political Science Review 13 (February 1919): 148-150.

F27   La France et la Guerre de l'Independance Americaine (1776-1783), by Capitaine Joachim Merlant. American Historical Review 24 (April 1919): 517-518.

F28   The League of Nations, by Mathias Erzberger; The Society of Nations, by T. J. Lawrence; The British Empire and a League of Peace, by G. B. Adams; and The Political Scene, by Walter Lippmann. Review, July 19, 1919, pp. 211-213.

F29   Life of John Marshall, vols. 3 and 4, by Albert J. Beveridge. Mississippi Valley Historical Review 6 (March 1920): 581-584.

F30   Lemuel Shaw, by Frederic Hathaway Chase. Mississippi Valley Historical Review 6 (March 1920): 584-585.

F31   The Monroe Doctrine and the Great War, by Arnold Bennett Hall; American Foreign Policy, by the Carnegie Endowment for International Peace; and An Introduction to the Peace Treaties, by Arthur Pearson Scott. Weekly Review, July 21, 1920, pp. 70-71.

F32   The Degradation of the Democratic Dogma, by Henry Adams. American Political Science Review 14 (August 1920): 507-509.

F33   The Rising Tide of Color Against White World-Supremacy, by Lothrop Stoddard. Unpartizan Review 14 (October-December 1920): 390-394.

F34   The Obligation of Contracts Clause of the United States Constitution, by Warren B. Hunting. American Political Science Review 14 (November 1920): 719-722.

F35   Problems of Law, Its Past, Present, and Future, by John Henry Wigmore; Judicial Reform, by John D. Works; and The Judiciary and the Constitution, by William M. Meigs. Weekly Review, November 10, 1920, pp. 449-450.

F36   International Law, A Treatise, by L. Oppenheim; International Law and the World War, by James Wilford Garner; The Equality of States in International Law, by Edwin DeWitt Dickinson. Weekly Review, March 2, 1921, pp. 202-204.

F37   Freedom of Speech, by Zechariah Chafee, Jr. Weekly Review, March 23, 1921, pp. 277-280.

F38   Popular Misgovernment in the United States, by Aldred B. Cruikshank; and Democracy and the Human Equation, by Alleyne Ireland. Weekly Review, April 30, 1921, pp. 420-421.

F39   The United States of America: A Study in International Organization, by James Brown Scott. University of Pennsylvania Law Review 69 (May 1921): 393-394.

F40   Selected Legal Papers, by Oliver Wendell Holmes. Weekly Review, July 16, 1921, pp. 61-62.

F41   Woodrow Wilson and his Work, by William E. Dodd. American Historical Review 27 (January 1922): 334-337.

F42   The American Philosophy of Government, Essays, by Alpheus Henry Snow. American Political Science Review 16 (May 1922): 325-326.

F43   War Powers of the Executive in the United States, by Clarence A. Berdahl. American Political Science Review 16 (August 1922): 511-513.

F44   The Supreme Court in United States History,
           by Charles Warren. American Historical Review
           28 (October 1922): 134-136.

F45   Cases on International Law, edited by James
           Brown Scott. University of Pennsylvania Law
           Review 71 (January 1923): 197-199.

F46   The Control of Foreign Relations, by Quincy
           Wright. Harvard Law Review 36 (February
           1923): 499-503.

F47   The Constitution of the United States, by James
           M. Beck; and The Law of the American Constitu-
           tion, by Charles K. Burdick. Literary Review,
           March 24, 1923, p. 549.

F48   Life of Roger Brooke Taney, by Bernard C. Stein-
           er. American Historical Review 28 (April
           1923): 556-557.

F49   The Constitution of Canada, by W. P. M. Ken-
           nedy. Literary Review, August 25, 1923, p.
           925.

F50   The Law of the American Constitution, by
           Charles K. Burdick. Independent, September
           29, 1923, p. 143.

F51   The Law of the American Constitution, by Char-
           les K. Burdick. Michigan Law Review 22 (Novem-
           ber 1923): 84-88.

F52   Diplomatic Portraits, by W. P. Cresson. Lit-
           erary Review, January 26, 1924, p. 472.

F53   The American Revolution: a Constitutional
           Interpretation, by Charles Howard McIlwain.
           American Historical Review 29 (July 1924):
           775-778.

F54 Recent Changes in American Constitutional Theory, by John W. Burgess; The Constitution of the United States, by Frederick J. Stimson; Federal Centralization, by Walter Thompson; and The Constitution of the United States, by Robert Livingston Schuyler. Literary Review, September 13, 1924, pp. 4-5.

F55 The Elements of Jurisprudence, by Sir Thomas Erskine Holland. Columbia Law Review 24 (December 1924): 936.

F56 The Conduct of Foreign Relations Under Modern Democratic Conditions. American Journal of International Law 19 (January 1925): 229-231.

F57 The Supreme Court and Sovereign States, by Charles Warren. Princeton Alumni Weekly, March 4, 1925, pp. 504-505.

F58 The Renascence of International Law, by Manfred Nathan. University of Pennsylvania Law Review 73 (May 1925): 452-453.

F59 Congress, the Constitution and the Supreme Court, by Charles Warren. American Bar Association Journal 12 (March 1926): 170-172.

F60 The Usages of the American Constitution, by Herbert W. Horwill. American Political Science Review 20 (May 1926): 436-439.

F61 The Constitution at the Crossroads, by Edward A. Harriman. American Political Science Review 21 (February 1927): 194-196.

F62 Constitutional Problems Under Lincoln, by James G. Randall. American Political Science Review 21 (May 1927): 429-432.

F63 The State as Party Litigant, by Robert Dorsey Watkins. Political Science Quarterly 42 (June 1927): 308-310.

F64 Colorado River Compact, by Reuel Leslie Olson. National Municipal Review 16 (July 1927): 459-461.

F65 An Introduction to the Study of the American Constitution, by Charles E. Martin. American Historical Review 32 (July 1927): 929-930.

F66 The United States and France, Some Opinions on International Gratitude, edited by James Brown Scott. Political Science Quarterly 42 (September 1927): 482.

F67 The Living Constitution: A Confederation of the Realities and Legends of Our Fundamental Law, by Howard Lee McBain. American Political Science Review 22 (May 1928): 461-463.

F68 The Business of the Supreme Court, by Felix Frankfurter and James M. Landis. Political Science Quarterly 43 (June 1928): 272-274.

F69 American Citizenship as Distinguished from Alien Status, by Frederick A. Cleveland. National Municipal Review 17 (July 1928): 420-421.

F70 The Worker Looks at Government, by Arthur W. Calhoun. American Political Science Review 23 (May 1929): 504-505.

F71 Some Lessons from our Legal History, by William Searle Holdsworth. American Historical Review 35 (October 1929): 98-99.

F72 Principles of Judicial Administration, by W. F. Willoughby. American Political Science Review 23 (November 1929): 1007-1011.

F73 The Supreme Court of the United States, by Charles Evans Hughes. Yale Law Journal 39 (December 1929): 295-297.

F74   A Review of the Work of the Supreme Court of the United States for October Term 1928, by Gregory Hankin and Charlotte A. Hankin. University of Pennsylvania Law Review 78 (May 1930): 926-927.

F75   The Dissenting Opinions of Mr. Justice Holmes. American Political Science Review 24 (August 1930): 780.

F76   Tenure of Office Under the Constitution, by James Hart. National Municipal Review 20 (February 1931): 96.

F77   A Selection of Cases and Authorities on Constitutional Law, by Oliver P. Field. American Political Science Review 25 (May 1931): 459-460.

F78   The Public and Its Government, by Felix Frankfurter. Political Science Quarterly 47 (March 1932): 105-107.

F79   American Interpretations of Natural Law, by Benjamin Fletcher Wright, Jr. Columbia Law Review 32 (April 1932): 764-766.

F80   Constitutional Law, by E. C. S. Wade and C. Godfrey Phillips. Virginia Law Review 18 (June 1932): 917-919.

F81   Our Wonderland of Bureaucracy, by James M. Beck. University of Pennsylvania Law Review 81 (November 1932): 99-102.

F82   Government by Judiciary, by Louis D. Boudin. American Political Science Review 26 (December 1932): 1107-1108.

F83   Cases and other Authorities on Constitutional Law, by Walter F. Dodd. Mercer Beasley Law Review 2 (January 1933): 106-107.

F84   Legislative Regulation, by Ernst Freund. Co-
       lumbia Law Review 33 (March 1933): 554-555.

F85   Our Obsolete Constitution, by William Kay Wal-
       lace. American Political Science Review 27
       (June 1933): 473-474.

F86   Parliamentary Opinion of Delegated Legislation,
       by Chih-Mai Chen. University of Pennsylvania
       Law Review 82 (April 1934): 674.

F87   Judicial Control of the Federal Trade Commis-
       sion and the Interstate Commerce Commission,
       1920-1930, by Carl McFarland. American Politi-
       cal Science Review 28 (June 1934): 518-520.

F88   Treaties Defeated by the Senate, by W. Stull
       Holt. Mississippi Valley Historical Review
       21 (December 1934): 439-441.

F89   The Challenge to Liberty, by Herbert Hoover;
       New Frontiers, by Henry A. Wallace; Liberty
       Under Law and Administration, by Homer Cum-
       mings; and The House of Adam Smith, by Eli
       Ginzberg. Yale Law Journal 44 (January 1935):
       546-550.

F90   Administrative Legislation and Adjudication,
       by Frederick F. Blachley and Miriam E. Oatman;
       and Principles of Legislative Organization
       and Administration, by W. F. Willoughby. Uni-
       versity of Pennsylvania Law Review 83 (May
       1935): 933-936.

F91   Proceedings of the Maryland Court of Appeals:
       1695-1729, edited by Carroll T. Bond and Rich-
       ard B. Morris. Political Science Quarterly
       50 (June 1935): 312-313.

F92   World Politics and Personal Insecurity, by
       Harold D. Lasswell. Annals of the American
       Academy of Political and Social Science 181
       (September 1935): 188-189.

F93 The Need for Constitutional Reform, by William Yandell Elliot. Yale Law Journal 45 (November 1935): 185-186.

F94 The Effect of an Unconstitutional Statute, by Oliver P. Field. Cornell Law Quarterly 21 (December 1935): 197-198.

F95 A Constitutional History of the United States, by Andrew C. McLaughlin. American Historical Review 41 (January 1936): 348-351.

F96 Declaratory Judgments, by E. Borchard. University of Toronto Law Journal 1 (Lent Term 1936): 402-404.

F97 Roger B. Taney, by Carl Brent Swisher; and Roger B. Taney, Jacksonian Jurist, by Charles W. Smith, Jr. American Political Science Review 30 (April 1936): 372-373.

F98 The Symbols of Government, by Thurman W. Arnold. American Political Science Review 30 (June 1936): 581-583.

F99 The Foundations of American Diplomacy, 1775-1823, by Samuel Flagg Bemis. American Historical Review 41 (July 1936): 769-771.

F100 Storm Over the Constitution, by Irving Brant; Fifty-Five Men, by Fred Rodell; and Whose Constitution?: An Inquiry into the General Welfare, by Henry A. Wallace. New Republic, September 9, 1936, pp. 135-136.

F101 Storm Over the Constitution, by Irving Brant; and Whose Constitution?: An Inquiry into the General Welfare, by Henry A. Wallace. American Political Science Review 30 (October 1936): 981-983.

F102 State Interests in American Treaties, by Nicholas Pendleton Mitchell. Brooklyn Law Review 6 (October 1936): 126-128.

F103 The Story of the Supreme Court, by Ernest Sutherland Bates. New York Herald Tribune, October 18, 1936, sec. 10, p. 3.

F104 Nine Old Men, by Drew Pearson and Robert S. Allen. Survey Graphic 26 (March 1937): 156.

F105 Brandeis, by Alfred Lief. Yale Review 26 (March 1937): 590-592.

F106 Neither Purse nor Sword, by James M. Beck and Merle Thorp. Annals of the American Academy of Political and Social Science 191 (May 1937): 244.

F107 The Power to Govern, by Walton H. Hamilton and Douglass Adair. American Political Science Review 31 (December 1937): 1147-1149.

F108 State and National Power over Commerce, by F. D. G. Ribble. Washington University Law Quarterly 23 (December 1937): 142.

F109 The Influence of the American Bar Association on Public Opinion and Legislation, by M. Louise Rutherford. Public Opinion Quarterly 2 (January 1938): 153-155.

F110 Interpreting the Constitution, by William Draper Lewis. American Bar Association Journal 24 (August 1938): 655.

F111 The Folklore of Capitalism, by Thurman W. Arnold. American Political Science Review 32 (August 1938): 745-746.

F112 The Constitution of Canada, 1534-1937, by W. P. M. Kennedy. Canadian Historical Review 19 (December 1938): 414-416.

F113 The Rise of a New Federalism, by Jane Perry Clark. Survey Graphic 27 (December 1938): 618.

F114   Mr. Justice Holmes and the Supreme Court, by Felix Frankfurter. Harvard Law Review 52 (December 1938): 346-348.

F115   Lectures on the American Constitution, by Maurice Sheldon Amos. Annals of the American Academy of Political and Social Science 202 (March 1939): 216-217.

F116   The Contract Clause of the Constitution, by Benjamin Fletcher Wright, Jr. Annals of the American Academy of Political and Social Science 202 (March 1939): 217-218.

F117   Our Eleven Chief Justices, by Kenneth Bernard Umbreit. Survey Graphic 28 (March 1939): 241-242.

F118   The Constitution Reconsidered, edited by Conyers Read. New York University Law Quarterly Review 16 (May 1939): 674-676.

F119   Taxation of Government Bondholders and Employees, by the Department of Justice. University of Pennsylvania Law Review 87 (May 1939): 883-886.

F120   Power: A New Social Analysis, by Bertrand Russell. American Bar Association Journal 25 (July 1939): 569.

F121   An Autobiographical Sketch of John Marshall, written at the Request of Joseph Story and now printed for the First Time from the Original Manuscript preserved at the William L. Clements Library, together with a Letter from Chief Justice Marshall to Justice Story relating Thereto, edited by John Stokes Adams. American Historical Review 44 (July 1939): 927-928.

F122   Handbook of American Constitutional Law, by Henry Rottschaefer. Yale Law Journal 49 (April 1940): 1143-1146.

F123 Constitutionalism: Ancient and Modern, by Charles Howard McIlwain; and Constitutionalism and the Changing World, by Charles Howard McIlwain. Harvard Law Review 54 (January 1941): 533-535.

   Reprint: Entry A16.

F124 Holmes-Pollock Letters: The Correspondence of Mr. Justice Holmes and Sir Frederick Pollock, 1874-1932, edited by Mark DeWolfe Howe. American Historical Review 47 (April 1942): 563-565.

F125 Free Speech in the United States, Zechariah Chafee. Annals of the American Academy of Political and Social Science 221 (May 1942): 192-193.

F126 The Supreme Court and Judicial Review, by Robert K. Carr. Annals of the American Academy of Political and Social Science 223 (September 1942): 238-239.

F127 The Constitutional History of the United States, by Homer Carey Hockett. American Political Science Review 36 (October 1942): 954-955.

F128 The Growth of American Constitutional Law, by Benjamin F. Wright. Harvard Law Review 56 (November 1942): 484-487.

F129 A New Constitution Now, by Henry Hazlitt. Nation, December 5, 1942, pp. 624-625.

F130 Mr. Justice Holmes, by Francis Biddle. New York Times Book Review, December 13, 1942, pp. 2, 22.

F131 Federal Cooperation with the States Under the Commerce Clause, by J. E. Kallenbach; and The Amending of the Federal Constitution, by L. B. Orfield. University of Toronto Law Journal 5 (Lent Term 1943): 195-198.

F132   The Presidents and Civil Disorder, by Bennett Milton Rich. American Historical Review 49 (October 1943): 116-117.

F133   The Third-Term Tradition, by Charles W. Stein. American Political Science Review 38 (February 1944): 185.

F134   The Republic, by Charles A. Beard. Columbia Law Review 44 (March 1944): 283-285.

F135   U.S. Foreign Policy, Shield of the Republic, by Walter Lippmann. Theology Today 1 (July 1944): 259-262.

F136   American Constitutional Development, by Carl Brent Swisher. American Historical Review 50 (October 1944): 127-131.

F137   Our Civil Liberties, by Osmond K. Fraenkel. American Political Science Review 38 (December 1944): 1216-1218.

F138   The Role of the Supreme Court in American Government and Politics, 1789-1835, by Charles Grove Haines. Yale Law Journal 54 (December 1944): 168-172.

F139   The Free State, by D. W. Brogan; Freedom under Planning, by Barbara Wootton; and Freedom and Responsibility in the American Way of Life, by Carl L. Becker. Virginia Quarterly Review 22 (Spring 1946): 311-320.

F140   The Constitution and Civil Rights, by Milton R. Konvitz. American Political Science Review 42 (February 1948): 117-118.

F141   A Declaration of Legal Faith, by Wiley Rutledge. University of Pennsylvania Law Review 96 (June 1948): 910-914.

F142   The Press and the Constitution, 1931-1947,
        by J. Edward Gerald. Public Opinion Quarterly
        12 (Winter 1948-1949): 749-750.

F143   Congress on Trial, by James MacGregor Burns.
        New York Times Book Review, July 17, 1949,
        pp. 1, 24.

F144   The Commerce Clause in the Constitution of
        the United States, by M. Ramaswamy. Aryan
        Path 21 (February 1950): 83-85.

F145   State and Local Government in the United
        States, by Cullen B. Gosnell and Lynwood M.
        Holland. Emory University Quarterly 7 (June
        1951): 124-126.

F146   The Declaration of Independence and What It
        Means Today, by Edward Dumbauld. Cornell Law
        Quarterly 37 (Winter 1952): 342-345.

F147   The Court and the Constitution, by Owen J.
        Roberts. Harvard Law Review 65 (June 1952):
        1471-1473.

F148   Charles Evans Hughes, by Merlo J. Pusey.
        American Political Science Review 46 (December
        1952): 1167-1173.

F149   Triumph of the Eggheads, by Horace Coon.
        America, October 1, 1955, p. 20.

F150   Charles Evans Hughes and American Democratic
        Statesmanship, by Dexter Perkins. America,
        September 22, 1956, p. 597.

G
Writings About Corwin

G1   "The Meeting of the American Historical Associa-
       tion at Madison." <u>American Historical Review</u>
       13 (April 1908): 433-458.

    Mentions on page 448 Corwin's participation in a
discussion on the teaching of constitutional law and
history.

G2   "The Constitution is Always Changing." <u>Wol-
       verine</u>, August 18, 1910, p. 1.

    Reports on Corwin's speech at the University of
Michigan on the evolution of judicial doctrines. Corwin
proposes that constitutional law is opening to broader
interpretations, particularly regarding the meaning of
"due process."

G3   "The Meeting of the American Historical Associa-
       tion at Indianapolis." <u>American Historical
       Review</u> 16 (April 1911): 453-475.

    Mentions on page 463 that Corwin presented a paper
on the Dred Scott Case, later published as the article
listed at Entry D11.

G4   "Edward S. Corwin: Critic of American Constitu-
       tional Theory." <u>Green Bag</u> 26 (October 1914):
       435-439.

Reviews many of Corwin's early writings and illustrates his unique theories. Corwin is praised for his modern thinking and original perspectives on constitutional history. The article further includes some biographical information and a photograph of the youthful Professor.

G5   "Says President Has Power to Supply Navy Convoy." New York Herald, March 6, 1917, p. 12.

Reports Corwin's belief that President Wilson has the constitutional authority to detail naval vessels as convoys for American merchant ships entering war zones. Wilson had concluded that he lacked the power without congressional approval. See Entries G6-G7.

G6   "Says Convoys are Legal." New York Times, March 6, 1917, p. 2.

Similar to the article listed at Entry G5.

G7   "Cites 'Armed Ship' Precedent for U.S." New York Sun, March 7, 1917, p. 2.

Similar to the article listed at Entry G5.

G8   "R.O.T.C. Announcement." Daily Princetonian, March 5, 1918, p. 1.

Lists Corwin as a staff instructor in the R.O.T.C. program. The Professor known as "the General" is officially given the rank of lieutenant.

G9   "The Freedom of the Seas." American Review of Reviews 59 (February 1919): 196-197.

Reports on Corwin's article listed at Entry D29 and includes extensive excerpts from it.

G10   Adams, George Burton. [Letter to the Editor:] "Professor Corwin on the Covenant." Review, August 2, 1919, pp. 254-256.

Responds to Corwin's article listed at Entry D32 and expands on his arguments about the Covenant of the League of Nations. See Entry E17.

G11   "Edward S. Corwin." In The New Historians:
        A Booklet About the Authors of the Chronicles
        of America, p. 25. New York: Yale University
        Press, 1920.

Provides a brief summary of Corwin's credentials with
reference to his authorship of the book listed at Entry
A5.1.

G12   Miller, David Hunter. [Letter to the Editor:]
        "Senate Opposition." New York Times, September
        17, 1920, p. 10.

Responds to Corwin's letter listed at Entry E19 and
concludes that Senate opposition to the Treaty of Versailles "is based on bitter and unreasoning personal
hatred of Woodrow Wilson." See Entry E20.

G13   "The Week." Harvey's Weekly, October 23, 1920,
        pp. 18-19.

Mentions at page 18 Corwin's criticism of President
Wilson's remarks on the Balkan States in relation to
the League of Nations.

G14   "Does Congress Want to Tax All Incomes?" New
        York World, January 26, 1923, p. 12.

Quotes from Corwin's article listed at Entry D48 in
an editorial arguing that the Sixteenth Amendment allows
Congress to tax income from state and municipal bonds.
The newspaper urges Congress to simply impose the tax
and allow the Supreme Court to decide the issue, rather
than making the specific matter the subject of a constitutional amendment.

G15   "Specially Trained Judiciary is Urged." New
        York Times, November 4, 1923, sec. 11, p. 15.

Quotes Corwin at length on his suggestion for a
tenured and specially-trained judiciary. He criticizes
the training provided by law schools and suggests that
psychologists should perhaps have veto power over judicial nominations.

G16   "Congress Has Power To Tax Income on Municipal
        Bonds." New York Tribune, January 27, 1924,
        sec. 4, p. 20.

Reports on the publication of Corwin's article listed at Entry D55 and sets forth his basic arguments that Congress has the power under the Sixteenth Amendment to tax income from state and municipal bonds.

G17   "Has Tax-Exemption Cure." New York Times, January 28, 1924, p. 26.

Reports on Corwin's article listed at Entry D55.

G18   "Tax-Exempts Already Illegal, Argues Noted Jurisprudent." Christian Science Monitor, February 12, 1924, p. 6.

Reports on Corwin's article listed at Entry D55 and reveals that Corwin wrote to the newspaper with his beliefs that a specific constitutional amendment permitting taxes on municipal bonds would be defeated, and that the Sixteenth Amendment should not be given any retroactive application.

G19   "Due Regard For The Federal Constitution." Sacramento Bee, September 10, 1924, p. 26.

Maintains that popular respect for the Constitution should be given not only to the written instrument but also to current interpretations of it. The editorial cites Corwin for the principle that the Constitution's meaning depends on judicial decisions.

G20   "Beveridge Upholds Powers of Courts." New York Times, January 21, 1925, p. 2.

Describes the meeting of the Lawyers Club of New York, at which former Senator Albert J. Beveridge and Corwin spoke on judicial review. Corwin's speech is printed as the articles listed at Entries D60 and D61.

G21   Powell, Thomas Reed. "Comment on Mr. Corwin's Paper." American Political Science Review 19 (May 1925): 305-308.

Analyzes Corwin's article listed at Entry D63 and criticizes Corwin's means of achieving national supremacy, without objecting to Corwin's basic thesis.

G22   "Tennessee Law is Unconstitutional." Princeton
           Herald, July 16, 1925, pp. 1-2.

Provides Corwin's analysis of the Scopes trial regarding the teaching of evolution in Tennessee schools.
Corwin concludes that the prohibition against teaching
evolution violates the Tennessee Constitution and the
First Amendment of the United States Constitution.

G23   "Princeton Teachers Stand with Scopes." New
           York Times, July 18, 1925, p. 2.

Presents Corwin's view that the law prohibiting the
teaching of non-biblical doctrines of creation violates
the United States Constitution as well as the Tennessee
Constitution.

G24   "Corwin Upholds Lectures as Being Useful Meth-
           od." Daily Princetonian, February 2, 1926,
           pp. 1, 4.

Examines Corwin's perspective on lectures as a teaching method. The Professor emphasizes that lectures are
the synthesis of long reflection, although their value
is often not clear to students. So Corwin has reduced
the number of lectures in his Constitutional Interpretation course from two to one, and he continues using
lectures to highlight assigned readings.

G25   "Corwin Upholds Stand of Coolidge on Liquor:
           Political Authority Defends Constitutionality
           of President's Prohibition Action." Daily
           Princetonian, May 25, 1926, p. 3.

Announces Corwin's support of President Coolidge's
order to employ state agents by the federal government
for enforcing Prohibition. See Entry G26.

G26   "Corwin Thinks Order Legal." New York Times,
           May 26, 1926, p. 2.

Similar to the article listed at Entry G25.

G27   "Professor Corwin Criticizes Decision." New
           York Times, October 27, 1926, p. 29.

Reports that Corwin objects to the recent Supreme
Court decision allowing the president to remove executive
officers. Corwin observes that if the removal power
is an inherent "executive power," it prevents Congress
from securing the tenure of civil servants.

G28   "How To Reduce Crime." Atlanta Journal, July
           17, 1927, p. 15.

Reveals Corwin's proposals for reducing crime. He
describes prosecution difficulties stemming from extra-
dition, criminal organizations, and the availability
of firearms. Corwin suggests that judges be allowed
greater power in criminal cases, and he supports capital
punishment.

G29   "Prof. Corwin Says Orient is Restless." Daily
           Princetonian, April 23, 1929, pp. 1, 3.

Offers observations by Corwin of China's political
and economic conditions following Corwin's year in
Peking. The Professor notes political turmoil in India,
the Philippines, and China, and he underscores the
serious poverty and famine in northern China. Corwin
gives compliments to the success of Yenching University
and to the Chinese officials who studied at Princeton.

G30   "A Princeton Professor on Yenching." Peking
           News 8 (May 1929): 8.

Includes Corwin's comments made upon leaving Yenching
University to return to Princeton. Corwin writes fondly
of the harmony at Yenching and the satisfaction donors
can receive by "backing a winner."

G31   "Federal System Held China's Needs." New York
           Times, May 5, 1929, sec. 2, p. 4.

Details Corwin's impressions of China after his term
as a visiting lecturer at three Chinese universities.
Corwin is interviewed about China's government, military,
and future. He believes that a strong national government is necessary, and that the government in Nanking
is best suited to the task.

G32   "China's Problems Called One of Economics."
           New York World, June 2, 1929, sec. 6, p. 12.

Reveals Corwin's observations about China following his year in Peking. The Professor is interviewed in detail about China's hopes for a unified government and strong economy, but he apparently recognizes the tremendous challenges for the country. Corwin suggests that China adopt a federal system and divide the nation into a North and South China. He recognizes, however, that "the Chinese are justifiably loath to adopt this solution because of the constant menace of foreign powers."

G33   Andrews, Paul Shipman. [Letter to the Editor:] "There Exists a No-Man's Land in Electric Rate Regulation." New York Times, July 6, 1930, sec. 3, p. 6.

Responds to Corwin's letter listed at Entry E27 and concludes that state and federal governments have limited powers to set electricity rates.

G34   "Prof. Corwin Says Dry Law Will Be Upheld." New York American, December 18, 1930, p. 6, late city and final editions.

Sets forth Corwin's theories for the validity of the Eighteenth Amendment. Corwin implies that the Amendment's ratification may have been deficient in some respects, but is nevertheless valid. See Entry G35.

G35   "Prof. Corwin Calls Clark View Wrong." New York Sun, December 18, 1930, p. 2, complete final edition.

Similar to the article listed at Entry G34.

G36   "Decision is Ignored by Jersey Dry Chief." New York Times, December 18, 1930, pp. 1, 17.

Includes Corwin's reaction to New Jersey's enforcement of Prohibition following a lower court decision against the constitutionality of the Eighteenth Amendment. Corwin predicts that the Supreme Court will overrule the decision.

G37   "Students Gather for International Relations Parley." Durham Morning Herald, February 27, 1931, sec. 1, pp. 1, 9.

Reports on Corwin's speech, "The Foreign Relations of China," given at a student conference on international relations at Duke University. Corwin traces China's development from Japan's victory in 1895 down through the contemporary status of Chinese-American relations. The Professor cautions that the threat of communism darkens China's future.

G38   Princeton in the Great War. Princeton: Princeton University, The Office of the Secretary, 1932.

Mentions at page 590 Corwin's activities during World War One. Professor Corwin served on the Committee on Public Information in Washington in 1917 and was a co-editor of the book listed at Entry B2. He also was an instructor in Princeton's Summer Military Course from June to August 1918.

G39   "Fights Ban on Jobs for Alien Students." New York Times, October 10, 1932, p. 17.

Presents Corwin's belief that a ruling by the Secretary of Labor prohibiting some foreign students from obtaining employment is unconstitutional.

G40   "Defeat of Drys on Beer Test in High Court Predicted by Prof. Corwin of Princeton." New York Times, March 20, 1933, p. 3.

Quotes Corwin's prediction that the Supreme Court would accept any reasonable judgment of Congress allowing sales of low-alcohol beer during Prohibition.

G41   "Seventeen Little Deans." Princeton Alumni Weekly, June 9, 1933, p. 774.

Summarizes Corwin's background and status as a popular teacher, accomplished scholar, and possible appointee to the Supreme Court.

G42   "The Power of Removal." New York Times, September 20, 1933, p. 20.

Addresses the issue of a president's power to remove executive officers and turns to Corwin's suggestion that the removal power can vary depending on the character of the office in issue.

G43   "The President's Power of Removal." <u>New York Times</u>, October 10, 1933, p. 20.

Similar to the article listed at Entry G42.

G44   "Professor Corwin's Letter." <u>Daily Princetonian</u>, October 11, 1933, p. 2.

Responds to Corwin's letter listed at Entry E29. The editorial argues that the Politics Department might permit its students who are simultaneously enrolled in the School of Affairs to study other topics, but the department does not encourage such diversity.

G45   "NRA Constitutional, Prof. Corwin Says." <u>New York Times</u>, November 7, 1933, p. 3.

Expresses Corwin's belief that the National Industrial Recovery Act is constitutional under the Commerce Clause and Due Process Clause. Corwin presents his views in a speech at Princeton, where he describes the NRA's constitutionality as a test of "the capacity of the Constitution to absorb a revolution."

G46   "Constitution vs. Constitutional Law." <u>America</u>, November 25, 1933, pp. 169-170.

Examines Corwin's belief that the constitutionality of New Deal legislation depends on the Constitution's ability to "absorb a Revolution." The editorial rejects that notion and suggests that the United States must either adopt a new constitution or return to the Constitution's original meaning.

G47   "N.R.A. Effect on Nation Called Revolutionary." <u>Los Angeles Times</u>, January 7, 1934, sec. 1, p. 9.

Reports on Corwin's speech published as the article listed at Entry D87 and quotes Corwin describing the National Industrial Recovery Act as a "constitutional revolution" because of its effects on the balance of powers among the federal government branches.

G48   NRA Is Scored and Defended on Consumers: Labor Leaders Attack Its 'Inadequacies'." <u>New York Times</u>, January 7, 1934, sec. 2, pp. 1, 6.

Includes Corwin's beliefs about the effect of the National Recovery Administration on the American Constitutional system, as discussed at a meeting of the American Academy of Political and Social Science. Corwin's speech is published as the article listed at Entry D87.

G49   "U.S. 'Revolution' Under New Deal Cited by Experts." Philadelphia Public Ledger, January 7, 1934, pp. 1, 8.

Reviews speeches made by Corwin and others at a conference sponsored by the American Academy of Political and Social Science. Corwin's speech is published as the article listed at Entry D87.

G50   "Professor Corwin on Minnesota Case." New York Times, January 11, 1934, p. 16.

Presents Corwin's analysis that the Supreme Court's reliance on emergency circumstances in upholding a state statute similar to New Deal legislation is not a limit on the viability of Roosevelt's program.

G51   "Dr. Corwin at Yale." Princeton Alumni Weekly, April 6, 1934, p. 600.

Announces Corwin's lecture series at Yale University, later published as the book listed at Entry A9.

G52   "Watch National Expenditures, States Corwin." New Haven Journal-Courier, April 13, 1934, p. 15.

Reports on the last of Corwin's lectures at Yale University presented by the Storrs Foundation. He spoke of the lack of constraint on federal spending and the need for some control to avoid bankruptcy. The lectures are published as the book listed at Entry A9.

G53   "Job-Insurance Plan Fought by Labor Leaders." New York Herald Tribune, February 18, 1935, p. 30.

Lists Corwin among those labor leaders, welfare workers, editors, and professors objecting to an unemployment insurance program proposed by the Roosevelt administration. Opponents criticize tax remissions and favor a federal subsidy.

G54   "Tracking a Quotation to Its Lair." <u>Christian</u>
             <u>Science Monitor</u>, March 9, 1935, p. 16.

Reviews the origin and later uses of Chief Justice
Hughes's expression: "The Constitution is what the
judges say it is." The issue emerged from Corwin's
reference to the quotation in his book listed at Entry
A9. The writer criticizes Corwin's use of the quotation
out of context.

G55   "Discovery of Notes Kept by Framer Throws New
             Light on U.S. Constitution." <u>Princeton Herald</u>,
             August 9, 1935, p. 1.

Presents Corwin's analyis of the importance of newly
discovered notebooks kept by John Lansing, Jr. while
serving as a delegate to the Constitutional Convention.
Corwin remarks that the Lansing notes support theories
that the framers desired a strong central government,
in contrast to the posture of the Supreme Court in 1935.

G56   "Highest Court Urged to Get Lansing Notes."
             <u>New York Times</u>, August 11, 1935, sec. 2, p. 3.

Announces Corwin's conclusion that the Lansing notes
from the Constitutional Convention are more accurate
than others, and that they reveal inconsistencies between
the framers' intent and recent Supreme Court decisions.

G57   "Legal Anarchy Laid to U.S. Court Rulings."
             <u>New York World-Telegram</u>, December 27, 1935,
             p. 2.

Includes Corwin's belief that the jurisdiction of
federal courts probably cannot be limited in a manner
that prevents review of constitutional issues. His
statement came during criticism of the Supreme Court's
rejection of New Deal legislation.

G58   Clapper, Raymond. "Ickes Expected to Return
             Fire Sunday on Smith Speech." <u>Washington Daily</u>
             <u>News</u>, January 24, 1936, p. 2.

Quotes Corwin's criticism of the Supreme Court in
his article listed at Entry D97 and likens his objections
to those of "ignorant persons, who don't know anything
about law. . . ."

G59   "The Court And The People." Cincinnati En-
           quirer, February 9, 1936, p. 6.

Reviews Corwin's response to the Supreme Court's
rejection of New Deal legislation. The article states
that Corwin favors the abolition of some of the legislation, but that he desires a constitutional interpretation responding to modern needs and allowing increased
federal powers.

G60   Lawrence, David. "Today in Washington: Guffey
           Act Issue Considered Reargument of Imperfectly
           Settled NRA Questions." New York Sun, March
           13, 1936, p. 17.

Examines in detail the government's arguments in the
Guffey Coal Case, which reviewed the constitutionality
of New Deal legislation regulating sales and prices.
The article focuses on Corwin's assistance in the case
and his position that the Commerce Clause grants Congress
authority to regulate activities related to interstate
shipment or sales of goods.

G61   Parton, Lemuel F. "Dr. Corwin of Princeton
           Was a Confrere of Woodrow Wilson." New York
      .   Sun, March 16, 1936, p. 29.

Summarizes Corwin's credentials in reference to his
collaboration with Assistant Attorney General John
Dickinson in preparation of the brief in the Guffey Coal
Case.

G62   "Judiciary." Time, March 23, 1936, p. 23.

Mentions Corwin's role in the Guffey Coal Case. The
article offers generous background on the case, examines
the parties' arguments, and reports on the arguments
before the Supreme Court.

G63   "Supreme Court Decisions Vary With Personnel."
           Schenectady Gazette, April 22, 1936, p. 4.

Reports on Corwin's appearance at a public forum held
at Union College and sponsored by the Laymen's League
of the First Unitarian Society. Corwin commented that
Supreme Court decisions reflect "judicial custom, the
trend of the times, the theories of its members or the
theories of noted jurists of the past" rather than strict
constitutional construction.

G64   "High Court Rulings on Acts of Congress and
         Critics Of Central Government Hit by Princeton
         Professor." Philadelphia Record, April 25,
         1936, sec. 2, p. E13.

Reports on Corwin's speech published as the article
listed at Entry D99 and Corwin's induction as a new member of the American Philosophical Society.

G65   "Noted Authorities to Present Views." Daily
         Princetonian, May 9, 1936, p. 9.

Announces the Constitutional Forum scheduled for that
day as part of the Harvard-Yale-Princeton Conference.
Scheduled liberal speakers were Corwin and Assistant
Attorney General John Dickinson. Conservative speakers
were New York attorneys Arthur A. Ballantine and Raoul
Desvernine.

G66   "Social Weal Held Guiding Public Aim." New
         York Times, May 10, 1936, sec. 1, p. 39.

Reports on the third annual Harvard-Yale-Princeton
round-table conference on government at which Corwin
called for a liberal constitutional interpretation and
declared that the Supreme Court was not functioning.

G67   "Corwin to Receive Degree at Harvard Tercen-
         tenary." Daily Princetonian, May 28, 1936,
         Special Bulletin, p. 1.

Announces Corwin's selection as a recipient of an
honorary degree from Harvard. The school conferred
sixty-six such degrees at its tercentenary celebration,
and Corwin presented a paper later published as the
article listed at Entry D102.

G68   Lyons, Louis M. "The World's Wise Men."
         Boston Globe, June 19, 1936, p. 20.

Announces Corwin's planned visit to Harvard University
as part of the school's tercentenary proceedings. The
article reviews Corwin's career, particularly his outspoken objections to Supreme Court rulings on New Deal
legislation, and it concludes that Corwin is a prospec-
tive appointee to the Court.

G69   "200 Attorneys at Bar Association Gathering
           Saturday." <u>Geneva Daily Times,</u> June 29, 1936,
           p. 7.

Reports on Corwin's speech before the Federation of
Bar Associations of Western New York meeting at Hobart
College. Corwin presented the "liberal view" of contemporary legislative trends on constitutional law. He
emphasized the need for change and adaptation for the
Constitution to survive, and the need for the government
to institute business regulations.

G70   "Back to the Constitution." <u>St. Louis Star-
           Times,</u> August 31, 1936, p. 2.

Contrasts Corwin's scholarly and liberal attitudes
about the Constitution with the economic and conservative
views espoused by the American Bar Association. The
editorial applauds Corwin's thesis, set forth in the
book listed at Entry A10, that contemporary Court rulings
are a restrictive reversal of Chief Justice Marshall's
views.

G71   Taft, Robert A. "Sidestepping the Constitu-
           tion." <u>Review of Reviews</u> 94 (September 1936):
           34-37.

Criticizes the New Deal and its effects on free enter-
prise. Taft specifically attacks Corwin's "sweeping
attempt to justify the New Deal" and efforts of the Roosevelt administration to alter constitutional principles.

G72   "Clarified View of Constitution Declared Need."
           <u>Christian Science Monitor,</u> September 9, 1936,
           sec. 2, pp. 9, 11.

Reports on Corwin's speech published as the article
listed at Entry D102 and notes that the Constitution
is a symbol for all persons, but an instrument for few.
The article concludes that slavery and business interests
left the largest impact on the Constitution's provisions
for national powers.

G73   "Carving 'Errors' On Supreme Court Building
           Debated." <u>Washington Evening Star,</u> September
           9, 1936, sec. 1, pp. 1-2.

Reports on Corwin's statements in a speech criticizing the relief depictions on the new Supreme Court doors. Corwin describes one panel as showing Justice Marshall handing the Marbury v. Madison decision to Justice Story, even though Story joined the Court nine years after the Marbury ruling. Corwin says another panel shows King John signing the Magna Carta, "although John probably could not write. . . ."

G74   Barnes, Joseph. "Constitutional Crisis Looms, Harvard Hears." New York Herald Tribune, September 10, 1936, p. 25.

Reports on Corwin's speech published as the article listed at Entry D102 and emphasizes the need to view the Constitution as an instrument of current needs not merely as a symbol of the past.

G75   MacDonald, James. "Says Constitution Needs Enlarging." New York Times, September 10, 1936, p. 14.

Reports on Corwin's speech published as the article listed at Entry D102.

G76   "Panels Refute Criticism." Washington Evening Star, September 10, 1936, sec. 2, p. 1.

Provides photographs of the disputed Supreme Court door panels and explains that Corwin's criticism may not be justified.

G77   "The Shirt of Nessus." Washington Daily News, September 11, 1936, p. 22.

Quotes from Corwin's speech published as the article listed at Entry D102 and compliments Corwin for his willingness to criticize the Supreme Court's rejection of New Deal legislation.

G78   Ginzburg, Benjamin. [Letter to the Editor:] "Cites Guide Book on Marshall-Story Panel." Washington Evening Star, September 15, 1936, sec. 1, p. 10.

Contributes to Corwin's vindication regarding the confusion about the depiction of Justices Marshall and Story on the Supreme Court doors. The writer refers to government guides and other literature describing the panel as Marshall handing the Marbury decision to Story.

G79   "Liberals to Have Corwin as Champion in Final
           Student-Faculty Forum." Daily Princetonian,
           October 29, 1936, p. 1.

Announces Corwin's appearance that night speaking in support of Franklin Roosevelt's re-election in a student-faculty debate.

G80   Bours, W. A. III and Shirk, J. S.   "'Sunflower
           Has Gone to Seed,' Claims Corwin, Who Sees
           Roosevelt as Having Done 'Good Job'." Daily
           Princetonian, October 29, 1936, pp. 1, 6.

Expresses Corwin's reasons for supporting Franklin Roosevelt in the 1936 election. Among his reasons is confidence that "if re-elected he won't be thinking of another term in the White House. . . ." In a premonition of the Court-packing proposal, Corwin sympathizes with Lincoln for having to increase the Supreme Court's size to meet Civil War demands.

G81   Memorandum of the Special Committee on the
           Constitution. Special Committee Memorandum,
           Number One. Washington: National Policy Com-
           mittee, 1937.

Sets forth the Committee's analyses regarding New Deal constitutional issues after meeting at the Brookings Institution in February 1937. Committee members included Corwin, Dean Acheson, Thurman Arnold, Charles Clark, and Robert Cushman. Court-packing was an immediate issue, and despite Corwin's chairmanship of the commit-tee, the group soundly criticized Roosevelt's proposal. The pamphlet briefly examines proposed constitutional amendments and suggestions for reversing the Supreme Court's conservative rulings.

G82   "The Nation's Honor Roll for 1936." Nation,
           January 2, 1937, p. 7.

Includes Corwin among those persons who "deserve the applause of their countrymen." Corwin is noted for his Harvard Tercentenary address, published as the article listed at Entry D102. See Entry G83.

G83   "An Honor Roll for 1936." Progressive, January 9, 1937, p. 7.

Reprints the article listed at Entry G82.

G84   "Savant Indorses F.D.R. Court Plan." Atlanta Constitution, February 8, 1937, pp. 1, 3.

Interviews Corwin on the Court-packing proposal. Corwin was participating in the Institute of Citizenship sponsored by Emory University, and he expressed immediate support for the president's plan. Much of the article centers on Corwin's dismissal of allegations that the plan is indicative of a Roosevelt "dictatorship."

G85   "Corwin Favors Court Reforms." New York Times, February 8, 1937, p. 6.

Reports on Corwin's sympathy with President Roosevelt on the Court-packing plan.

G86   "Corwin for Court Reform." New York Times, February 9, 1937, p. 4.

Expresses Corwin's urgings for mandatory retirement of all federal judges at age seventy.

G87   "Question of Dictators." Raleigh News and Observer, February 9, 1937, p. 4.

Quotes Corwin's statements made in Atlanta immediately upon President Roosevelt's announcement of the Court-packing proposal. The article adopts Corwin's view that the plan is not the creation of dictatorship, but rather is a response to dictatorship by the Supreme Court.

G88   Bours, W. A. III. "New Roosevelt Bill to Remodel Courts Approved by Corwin." Daily Princetonian, February 12, 1937, p. 1.

Sets forth Corwin's announcement of support for Roosevelt's Court-packing plan. Corwin urges an age limit of seventy for the justices and declines to discuss prospects of his possible appointment to the Court.

G89   White, Thomas Raeburn. [Letter to the Editor:] "Danger Seen in Court Plan." New York Times, February 26, 1937, p. 20.

Criticizes Corwin's article listed at Entry D119 and the Court-packing proposal. The writer dismisses many historical precedents cited by Corwin.

G90   "Corwin Assails Court View of Constitution." New York Sun, March 17, 1937, p. 16.

Summarizes Corwin's prepared statement before the Senate Judiciary Committee in the Court-packing hearing. See Entry D123.

G91   "Most Justices Wrong on Constitution, Professor Tells Senate's Hearing." New York World-Telegram, March 17, 1937, p. 2.

Similar to the article listed at Entry G90.

G92   Lincoln, G. Gould. "Educator Views 'Economic Bias' Swaying Court." Washington Evening Star, March 17, 1937, sec. A, pp. 1, 5.

Reports on Corwin's appearance before the Senate Judiciary Committee in support of Court-packing. The article emphasizes Corwin's earlier disapproval of packing the Court and Corwin's criticism of constitutional amendments as a means of effecting changes. See Entry D123.

G93   "9 Justices Urged To State Views on Court Curb Plan." New York Herald Tribune, March 18, 1937, pp. 1, 13.

Reviews proceedings by the Senate Judiciary Committee on Court-packing, including Corwin's hearing and efforts by the committee to have Supreme Court justices testify. See Entry D123.

G94   Catledge, Turner. "Justices Pressed for Court
        Views." New York Times, March 18, 1937, p. 18.

Reports on Corwin's hearing on the Court-packing
proposal and highlights the conflict between Corwin's
support of Court-packing and his previous statements
against it. The details and quotations in this article
surpass information printed in the transcript. See Entry
D123.

G95   Albright, Robert C. "Corwin Urges 15-Judge
        Court With Three Functioning Panels." Wash-
        ington Post, March 18, 1937, pp. 1, 5.

Describes dramatically and elaborately Corwin's
appearance for three hours before the Senate Judiciary
Committee on Court-packing. The article portrays Corwin
as successfully deflecting harsh criticism from hostile
Senators and highlights Corwin's suggested division of
the Court into three separate panels. See Entry D123.

G96   "Live and Learn." New York Times, March 19,
        1937, p. 22.

Examines briefly Corwin's humility and willingness
to confess "I live and learn" in response to accusations
of changing his mind on Court-packing. See Entry D123.

G97   "Corwin vs. Consistency." Daily Princetonian,
        March 20, 1937, p. 2.

Compliments Corwin for his courage to admit in the
Senate hearing on Court-packing that he changed his mind
about the merits of the proposal. See Entry D123.

G98   "First Steps in Inconsistency." New York
        Times, March 21, 1937, sec. 4, p. 8.

Comments briefly on Corwin's Senate hearing on Court-
packing. See Entry D123.

G99   Corbin, John. [Letter to the Editor:] "An
        'Industrial Amendment'." New York Times, March
        22, 1937, p. 22.

Responds to Corwin's testimony at the Court-packing
hearing about the Court's becoming a "hybrid" body, per-
forming political and judicial functions.

G100   Bunn, Charles. "Discussion of Professor Cor-
            win's Paper." American Law School Review 8
            (April 1937): 705.

Responds to Corwin's article listed at Entry D124
and supports Corwin's thesis. See Entry G101.

G101   Curtis, Charles P., Jr. "Discussion of Pro-
            fessor Corwin's Paper." American Law School
            Review 8 (April 1937): 706-707.

Responds to Corwin's article listed at Entry D124
and analyzes judicial limits on federal supremacy. See
Entry G100.

G102   Bradley, Phillips. "The Constitution, the
            Court and the People." Social Education 1
            (April 1937): 235-242.

Examines the historical and theoretical underpinnings
of Roosevelt's Court-packing proposal, giving emphasis
to Corwin's analysis of the Constitution as an "instrument" and "symbol." Bradley concludes that Court-packing
is one of the least radical proposals for remedying
problems with the Supreme Court.

G103   [Letter to the Editor:] "Academic Freedom
            in Discussing the Supreme Court." Princeton
            Alumni Weekly, April 2, 1937, p. 550.

Criticizes Corwin's appearance at the Senate hearing
on Court-packing. The anonymous author argues that
Corwin gave Princeton a bad image by supporting the
president's plan.

G104   "Court Change Plan Debated in Pulpits." New
            York Times, April 5, 1937, p. 15.

Reports on Corwin's speech in support of Court-packing
as presented at a meeting of the New York Society for
Ethical Culture.

G105   Howden, Norman. "CIO Bearing in Court Ruling
            Cited." Rochester Democrat and Chronicle,
            April 15, 1937, p. 21.

Reports on Corwin's lecture at the University of Rochester, later published as the article listed at Entry D125. In an interview, Corwin says labor strikes underscored popular support for the Wagner Labor Relations Act and influenced its being upheld by the Court. Corwin confesses that the Wagner decision has changed attitudes about Court-packing, but he continues to advocate a retirement age of seventy with a twenty-one year maximum term on the bench.

G106   "Savant Talks About Court." Lexington Leader, June 15, 1937, p. 13.

Reports on Corwin's speech at the University of Kentucky, where he was on the summer school faculty. Corwin reviewed the Supreme Court's historical interpretations of the Commerce Clause down through recent decisions upholding New Deal legislation.

G107   "Finds U.S. Rule Is Built on Two Constitutions." Cleveland News, June 22, 1937, sec. 1, p. 8.

Reports briefly on Corwin's opening address at the Institute of Current Affairs at Western Reserve University. He spoke of constitutional law subject to opinions of the justices, leaving the Constitution itself as only the nucleus of the "working constitution."

G108   "Constitution Expert Talks at W.R.U. Forum." Cleveland Press, June 22, 1937, p. 2.

Similar to the article listed at Entry G107.

G109   Cunningham, L. W. "Random Comment." Colorado Springs Gazette & Telegraph, October 31, 1937, sec. 3, p. 4.

Responds to Corwin's letter listed at Entry E32 and offers controverting evidence "that Madison studied law diligently, but, owing to his shyness, he probably rarely appeared in court."

G110   "First Bar Lecture Stirs The Profession." Pittsburgh Legal Journal, December 15, 1937, p. 3.

Describes the December 14, 1937 meeting of the Allegheny County Bar Association at which Corwin delivered the paper published as the article listed at Entry D127.

G111   "The President's of the American Political Science Association, 1904-1938." American Political Science Review 32 (October 1938): frontispieces preceding page 1059.

Includes a photograph of Corwin.

G112   "An Unjust Quotation." New York Sun, November 8, 1938, p. 14.

Criticizes Corwin's use out of context of the following quotation by Charles Evans Hughes: "We live under a Constitution, but the Constitution is what the Judges say it is. . . ." See Entry G54.

G113   Lerner, Max. "Corwin and the Judicial Power." In Ideas are Weapons: The History and Uses of Ideas, pp. 228-234. New York: The Viking Press, 1939.

Reviews Corwin's book listed at Entry A11 and criticizes lightly the Professor's theories.

G114   Van Anda, Carr V. [Letter to the Editor:] "Congressional Power to Withdraw Privilege Denied." New York Times, February 19, 1939, sec. 4, p. 9.

Comments on Corwin's letter listed at Entry E34.

G115   Fox, Frederic E. "On the Campus." Princeton Alumni Weekly, June 6, 1939, pp. 772-773.

Publishes the Corwin verse of the Princeton "faculty song:" "Corwin is our judge supreme/All legal questions he can cream/But lawbooks do not mention style/So at his knickers we still smile." The article acknowledges an error in the ditty; Corwin discontinued wearing knickers three years before.

G116   "May Force Russia's Hand." New York Times, October 24, 1939, p. 6.

Explains Corwin's belief that Germany had the right to seize an American ship carrying contraband, and that taking the ship to Murmansk could compel the Soviet Union to clarify its relations with Germany.

G117   "Violations Laid to British." New York Times, November 22, 1939, p. 6.

Reports Corwin's announcement that British seizures of German exports in retaliation for German mine-laying in British waters violated international law and the rights of neutrals.

G118   "Madison Not a Lawyer." New York Times, December 3, 1939, sec. 4, p. 8.

Reports on Corwin's article listed at Entry D131.

G119   Holland, Laurence B. "Sale of Destroyers Attacked By Corwin in Letter to 'Times'." Daily Princetonian, October 14, 1940, p. 1.

Summarizes Corwin's letter listed at Entry E36.

G120   Krock, Arthur. "The Intelligentsia Here and Abroad United in Campaign." New York Times, October 15, 1940, p. 22.

Comments on Corwin's views of Roosevelt's third term and of his power to execute the Destroyer-Bases Agreement. Krock notes that Corwin is not following the political beliefs of most intellectuals.

G121   Davies, Lawrence E. "Congress Leaders Urged in Cabinet." New York Times, November 23, 1940, p. 19.

Reports on Corwin's speech at a meeting of the American Philosophical Society about his proposed cabinet comprising key members of Congress.

G122   Lerner, Max. "The Presidential Office: The Job in the White House." In Ideas for the Ice Age: Studies in a Revolutionary Era, pp. 386-389. New York: The Viking Press, 1941.

Reviews Corwin's book listed at Entry A12.1 and notes the constitutional analysis of the presidency, in contrast to a personalized or institutional view.

G123   American Philosophical Society Year Book, 1940. Philadelphia: American Philosophical Society, 1941.

Mentions at page 40 that Corwin received the Society's Franklin Medal on November 22, 1940.

G124   "The totalitarian state is a dangerous simplification of government, says authority." Los Angeles News, January 24, 1941, p. 23.

Reports on Corwin's series of lectures at Pomona College, published as the book listed at Entry A13.1. The article quotes Corwin extensively on the "revolution" in constitutional law and the challenge of balancing liberty and equality in governmental functions.

G125   Hogue, Fred. "Constitution Amending Declared Outmoded." Los Angeles Times, January 30, 1941, p. 11.

Reports on Corwin's lectures at Claremont, published as the book listed at Entry A13.1. Corwin spoke very critically of Franklin Roosevelt's Supreme Court appointees and of the New Deal's effects on constitutional law. He emphasized that the Court is permitting an active government to protect rights, resulting in an erosion of the "due process" limitation on Congress.

G126   "Corwin Writes 'Times' On Power of Congress." Daily Princetonian, March 3, 1941, p. 1.

Reports on Corwin's letter listed at Entry E38.

G127   "Professor Corwin Writes Volume About Presidency." Daily Princetonian, March 10, 1941, p. 1.

Reports publication of the book listed at Entry A12.1.

G128   Ruch, Walter W. "Stresses Freedom as Basis of Peace." New York Times, April 26, 1942, sec. 1, p. 25.

Reports that Corwin received the sixth Henry M. Phillips prize at a meeting of the American Philosophical Society for his book listed at Entry A12.1.

G129   "E. S. Corwin Gets Phillips Prize." New York Times, April 26, 1942, sec. 1, p. 42.

Similar to the article listed at Entry G128.

G130   American Philosophical Society Year Book, 1942. Philadelphia: American Philosophical Society, 1943.

Mentions at page 53 that Corwin received the Henry M. Phillips Prize on March 25, 1942; and mentions at page 57 that Corwin made a radio address on June 5, 1942 entitled "The Federal Idea, Especially as It Has Evolved in the United States."

G131   Labue, Frances B. "Prof. Corwin Believes John L. Lewis' Tactics Will Prove Detrimental to Labor in Long Run." Baton Rouge State-Times, May 7, 1943, p. 6B.

Presents Corwin's opposition to the labor tactics of John L. Lewis, whom Corwin describes as "a creation of Mr. Roosevelt." The Professor is generally critical of Roosevelt, and on the subject of a fourth term he says sarcastically: "considering the shape in which the country may very well be at the end of the third term, I don't think he deserves anything better."

G132   "The Two-Thirds Rule." New Republic, November 29, 1943, pp. 787-789.

Argues for a change of the two-thirds rule for Senate ratification of treaties. The article quotes Corwin on the difficulty of obtaining Senate consent for a constitutional amendment that would change the rule to require only a majority vote for ratification.

G133   Wright, Dupont. "DeKalb Rent Ceiling Case Lost by OPA." Atlanta Constitution, November 30, 1943, p. 5.

Reports on Corwin's participation in a Georgia trial in which the judge found sections of the Office of Price Administration law unconstitutional. Corwin appeared as a guest of the petitioner's attorney and advised the judge not to decide the constitutional issue until all administrative procedures were exhausted. The judge nevertheless dismissed the petitioner's action. In a separate interview Corwin gave his views on World War Two developments.

G134   Killheffer, Elvin H. [Letter to the Editor:] "Senate Consent Approved." New York Times, July 5, 1944, p. 16.

Responds to Corwin's letter listed at Entry E39 and argues that executive agreements deviate from constitutional procedure.

G135   The Evolution of Social Institutions in America. Princeton University Bicentennial Conferences, series 1, conference 4. Princeton: Princeton University, 1946.

Summarizes at pages 4-6 Corwin's participation in the conference held at Princeton University on October 7-9, 1946. Corwin's topic was "American Federalism-- Past, Present and Future." He spoke of changing concepts of federalism, from a "competitive" conception espoused by early Supreme Court decisions to the "cooperative" conception of the New Deal. Under the latter notion of federalism, the state and national governments work together to meet modern needs.

G136   "Corwin, Edward Samuel." In National Cyclopaedia of American Biography, Current Vol. G, p. 511. New York: James T. White & Company, 1946.

Presents a brief biography of Corwin, emphasizing his family history and professional career and detailing his roster of lectureships.

G137   Kauper, Paul G. "The William W. Cook Lectures on American Institutions: Delivered by Professor Edward Samuel Corwin, March 18-22, 1946." Michigan Alumnus Quarterly Review 52 (Summer 1946): 306-312.

Summarizes in substantial detail Corwin's lecture series at the University of Michigan published as the book listed at Entry A15. The article gives an informative description of the Cook Lectures and Corwin's qualifications, followed by a careful review of the critical points that Corwin discussed, such as Roosevelt's growing powers and the permanent transformation of the Constitution after the New Deal and World War Two.

G138   "Dinner to Honor Dr. Corwin." New York Herald Tribune, June 3, 1946, p. 9.

Announces Corwin's retirement and a dinner in his honor at Princeton.

G139   "Dr. Corwin, Retiring, Honor Guest Tonight." Daily Princetonian, June 3, 1946, p. 1.

Announces Corwin's retirement dinner and briefly describes the Professor's academic career.

G140   Dear, Ralph C. "Dr. E. S. Corwin Honored at Banquet; President Dodds and Many Others Speak." Daily Princetonian, June 4, 1946, p. 1.

Reports on the accolades and honors given to Corwin at his retirement dinner at Princeton.

G141   "Goodbye Now." Time, July 15, 1946, p. 70.

Announces briefly Corwin's retirement and describes him as one of the last four original preceptors, all retiring that year. The article further refers to Corwin as a "vigorous defender of Roosevelt's 1937 Court-packing plan."

G142   "Rear Guard of 'Preceptor Guys' Retires." Princeton Alumni Weekly, July 19, 1946, pp. 8-9.

Includes another Corwin verse to the Princeton "faculty song:" "Here's to Corwin, Edward S./In law he never has to guess;/He'll tell you briefly, so they say/The reasons for the U.S.A."

G143   Frank, Jerome. [Letter to the Editor:] "Judge
        Frank Replies." New York Times Book Review,
        June 1, 1947, p. 19.

Responds to Corwin's letter listed at Entry E40 and
criticizes Corwin's subjective view of history.

G144   "Decision on Study of Religion Scored." New
        York Times, October 15, 1948, p. 20.

Explains Corwin's objections to a Supreme Court decision prohibiting religious "released time" in public
schools. See Entries D152-D153 and G146-G147.

G145   Agnew, P. G. [Letter to the Editor:] "Unac-
        countable." New York Times Magazine, October
        24, 1948, p. 4.

Responds to Corwin's article listed at Entry D151
and criticizes his proposed cabinet comprising members
of Congress. The writer does not believe that Corwin's
proposal would cure the unaccountability and irrespon-
sibility of either the president or Congress.

G146   "Corwin Attacks Ruling In Champaign Case."
        Christian Century, October 27, 1948, p. 1133.

Reviews Corwin's criticism of a Supreme Court decision
restricting school religion classes, as reported in the
article listed at Entry G144.

G147   "Corwin scores McCollum decision." America,
        October 30, 1948, pp. 90-91.

Praises Corwin's speech opposing the Supreme Court
ruling against "released time" religious instruction
in public schools, emphasizing Corwin's belief that the
First Amendment "was never before interpreted to mean
that Congress could not support religion, provided it
did so without discrimination." See Entry G144.

G148   Krock, Arthur. "Powers of Presidency Stir
        Capital Debate." New York Times, February
        6, 1949, sec. 4, p. 3.

Analyzes the president's power in a tripartite government and refers to Corwin's book listed at Entry A12.3
for further examination.

G149   Sattong, Mrs. Philipp C. [Letter to the
        Editor:] "For Best Minds." New York Times
        Magazine, August 21, 1949, p. 4.

Responds to Corwin's article listed at Entry D155
and gives it light criticism about Congress's power to
declare war. The writer suggests that war is made by
foreign attacks, not by the American government. Thus,
the United Nations should become a world government to
prevent wars among nations.

G150   "Usurpations Laid to British Regime." New
        York Times, December 10, 1949, p. 15.

Reports on Corwin's attendance at the Third Natural
Law Institute and on his speech published as the essay
listed at Entry C23.

G151   "Electoral Reform." Washington Post, February
        19, 1950, sec. 2, p. 4.

Criticizes Corwin's support of the Lodge-Gosset Resolution to have electoral college members elected from
local districts. The editorial concludes that the peri-
odic creation of districts would be an unmanageable task
for Congress, and that the plan would discourage the
establishment of new and smaller parties.

G152   Krock, Arthur. "In The Nation: The Courts
        and the Secret Files Impasse." New York Times,
        March 30, 1950, p. 28.

Quotes Corwin on the subject of executive privilege
and immunity. Corwin suggests that the president should
use his pardoning power to prevent disclosure of secrets.

G153   Krock, Arthur. "In The Nation: When a Court
        Subpoenaed the President." New York Times,
        March 31, 1950, p. 30.

Quotes Corwin on the "give and take" of power by the
president and Congress on the issue of executive privilege.

G154   Reuschlein, Harold Gill. Jurisprudence--Its
        American Prophets: A Survey of Taught Juris-
        prudence (Indianapolis: Bobbs-Merrill Company,
        Inc., 1951).

Examines at pages 342-345 Corwin's contributions to jurisprudence, emphasizing his essay listed at Entries D71 and D72 and his book listed at Entry A16. Reuschlein notes that Corwin's jurisprudence does not search for true legal philosophy, but rather studies the effect of prevailing legal philosophy on society. The book surveys the development of American jurisprudence through brief studies of prominent theorists.

G155 Bliven, Bruce. "27 Who Believed in Justice." New Republic, October 22, 1951, pp. 13-15.

Sets forth a general background of the "Trenton Six" case in which six black men were sentenced to death on the basis of weak evidence surrounding a murder in Trenton, New Jersey. Corwin was co-chairman of the Princeton Committee for Defense of the Trenton Six, a group of 27 citizens supporting the defense of the accused.

G156 "Princeton Law Professor Defends Vatican Envoy." Catholic News, November 17, 1951, p. 9.

Quotes at length Corwin's letter listed at Entry E48.

G157 Van Dusen, Henry P. [Letter to the Editor:] "Vatican Embassy Opposed." New York Times, November 21, 1951, p. 24.

Responds to Corwin's letter listed at Entry E48 and criticizes President Truman's plans to open a Vatican embassy.

G158 "Dr. Corwin on Vatican envoy." America, November 24, 1951, p. 197.

Applauds Corwin's letter listed at Entry E48.

G159 "The Case of the Trenton Two." New York Times, November 28, 1951, p. 34.

Displays a full-page advertisement by the Committee for Defense of the Trenton Six, referred to at Entry G155 above, after the cases of only two of the defendants were on appeal.

G160   Howe, Mark de Wolfe. "Diplomacy, Religion, and the Constitution." Nation, January 12, 1952, pp. 28-30.

Responds to Corwin's letter listed at Entry E48 and criticizes Corwin's support for President Truman's right to send an ambassador to the Vatican.

G161   Kurzman, Peter H. "Corwin States Seizure Has Dubious Precedence." Daily Princetonian, April 22, 1952, p. 2.

Sets forth Corwin's opinion that President Truman's seizure of the steel industry is "both unprecedented and the contrary." Corwin distinguishes some historic parallels and urges Congress to define the president's powers in labor disputes in order to control presidential authority.

G162   "The Emeriti Professors." Princeton Alumni Weekly, April 25, 1952, pp. 11-23.

Describes the post-retirement activities of several Princeton professors, and sets forth at page 18 some of Corwin's teaching and scholarly achievements.

G163   Hermens, Ferdinand A. [Letter to the Editor:] "Reforming Government." New York Times, July 27, 1952, sec. 4, p. 8.

Comments favorably on Corwin's proposed cabinet comprising members of Congress and recommends it to the next administration.

G164   Vanderbilt, Arthur T. Foreword to 1953 Annual Survey of American Law, pp. vii-viii. Edited by Robert B. McKay. New York: New York University School of Law, 1953.

Includes a collection of essays on developments in the law during 1953. The volume, in an annual series, is dedicated to Corwin for his completion of the book listed at Entry B4.

G165   Lissner, Will. "Law Experts Say Truman Acted Beyond His Constitutional Right." New York Times, November 13, 1953, pp. 1, 14.

Reports the opinions of Corwin and others that former President Truman had no constitutional basis for non-compliance with a subpoena for appearance before the House of Representatives.

G166   "Leaders to Fight Bricker Proposal." New York Times, December 28, 1953, p. 3.

Announces Corwin's appointment as chairman of the Committee for Defense of the Constitution by Preserving the Treaty Power. The Committee opposes the Bricker Amendment which would restrict the president's treaty-making powers.

G167   Krock, Arthur. "Treaty-Making Reform by Senate Rules." New York Times, December 29, 1953, p. 22.

Comments on the committee described at Entry G166 and outlines alternative methods of curbing presidential power.

G168   "The Interventionists Hit the Warpath." Chicago Daily Tribune, January 4, 1954, sec. 1, p. 22.

Notes the irony of Corwin's opposition to the Bricker Amendment in light of his outspoken criticism of growing presidential powers. The editorial classifies Corwin among the "band of interventionists" opposing the amendment and thereby "arguing for a government without constitutional restraint."

G169   Krock, Arthur. "Some New Thinking on the Bricker Amendment." New York Times, January 5, 1954, p. 26.

Analyzes Senate debates regarding the Bricker Amendment, with emphasis on a provision prohibiting treaties that confer new legislative powers on Congress. Krock cites Corwin's contention that the provision could require approval of some treaties by each state.

G170   Abrams, Burt J. "Bricker Measure Is Called Isolationist by Prof. Corwin." Daily Princetonian, January 6, 1954, p. 1.

Outlines Corwin's objections to the Bricker Amendment, designed to restrict federal powers in international relations. Although he finds the proposal not entirely unjustifiable, he believes that it "would go too far and prevent the United States from making the type of treaties and international agreements that it has always made."

G171   White, William S. "Bricker Assails Eisenhower Role in Treaty Debate." New York Times, January 23, 1954, pp. 1-2.

Mentions Corwin's opposition to the Bricker Amendment and includes some criticism of the conflict between his opposition and his service to the government in preparing the book listed at Entry B4.

G172   "Group Here Fights Bricker Proposal." New York Times, February 4, 1954, p. 14.

Reports of a telegram sent to President Eisenhower by Corwin and other prominent members of the Committee for Defense of the Constitution, urging the president to oppose the Bricker Amendment.

G173   Kihss, Peter. "Experts Approve Timetable on Bias." New York Times, May 18, 1954, p. 18.

Reports Corwin's response to the Supreme Court's Brown v. Board of Education decision and the delayed implementation of desegregation. Corwin favors the delay until public reactions to the ruling can settle.

G174   Baker, Richard T. "Princeton Class Warned of Worry." New York Times, June 16, 1954, p. 28.

Reports on Corwin's receiving an honorary Doctor of Laws degree from Princeton University.

G175   "Citations for Corwin, Morey and Russell And Other Honorary Degree Recipients." Princeton Herald, June 16, 1954, pp. 2-3.

Mentions that Corwin received an honorary degree from Princeton University, and gives a brief sketch of his career at the school.

G176   "Court Test Expected On Red Outlaw Bill."
        New York Times, August 20, 1954, pp. 1, 7.

Includes Corwin's comments on the constitutionality
of an act of Congress outlawing the Communist Party.
Corwin believes that a constitutional challenge would
be difficult, even though political circumstances motivated passage of the measure.

G177   Brant, Irving. [Letter to the Editor.] Ameri-
        can Historical Review 60 (January 1955): 497.

Responds succinctly to Corwin's letter listed at Entry
E50.

G178   Krock, Arthur. "President Cuts Short Consti-
        tutional Debate." New York Times, January
        30, 1955, sec. 4, p. 3.

Examines Eisenhower's request for Congress's cooperation with sending forces to defend Formosa Strait. Krock
cites Corwin when underscoring the need for cooperation
between the two branches of government.

G179   "Group Here Sets Fight on Bricker Plan." New
        York Times, May 9, 1955, p. 16.

Reports on the committee described at Entry G166 and
its forthcoming presentation to the Senate Judiciary
Subcommittee.

G180   "3 College Heads Praise Decision." New York
        Times, June 1, 1955, p. 29.

Includes Corwin's reactions to the Supreme Court's
ruling that desegregation of schools occur as quickly
as possible. Corwin finds the ruling necessarily vague
until specific instances of segregation can be reviewed.

G181   Schlafly, J. F., Jr. [Letter to the Editor:]
        "The Bricker Amendment." New York Herald Tri-
        bune, June 4, 1955, p. 6.

Responds to Corwin's article listed at Entry D175
and argues in favor of the Bricker Amendment. Schlafly's
principal concern is the president's ability to make
private agreements that can ultimately supersede conflicting state laws.

G182   Kihss, Peter. "What Happens if a President
            Cannot Perform His Duties Is an Unsettled Ques-
            tion." New York Times, September 26, 1955,
            p. 15.

Includes Corwin's explanation of the uncertain possibilities during President Eisenhower's incapacity with
a heart ailment. Corwin urges legislation to clarify
procedures.

G183   Faber, Eberhard. "Corwin Asks New Law For
            Presidential Crises." Daily Princetonian,
            October 13, 1955, pp. 1, 3.

Explains the uncertainty of Nixon's constitutional
status during Eisenhower's hospitalization. Corwin calls
for legislation to define the vice president's role during presidential disability and to establish a panel
to judge when a president is able to discharge his
duties.

G184   "4 to Run Holmes Fund." New York Times, Janu-
            ary 10, 1956, p. 15.

Reports Corwin's appointment by President Eisenhower
to a four-year term on the Permanent Committee for the
Oliver Wendell Holmes Devise.

G185   Reston, James. "If the President Runs." New
            York Times, February 28, 1956, p. 19.

Quotes from the book listed at Entry A20 on the president's health and on succession to the presidency.

G186   Krock, Arthur. "In The Nation: Unsung Valor
            of a House Subcommittee." New York Times,
            April 13, 1956, p. 24.

Refers to Corwin's proposals and suggestions on presidential inability and succession.

G187   Huston, Luther A. "History of Court to Honor
            Holmes." New York Times, April 15, 1956, p.
            80.

Reviews the formation, structure, and goals of the Permanent Committee for the Oliver Wendell Holmes Devise. Corwin was a member of the fund's committee assigned to write a history of the Supreme Court. See Entry G184.

G188   "Wilson's Career as President Will Be Evaluated by Corwin." Daily Princetonian, April 18, 1956, p. 1.

Announces Corwin's lecture on "Woodrow Wilson and the Presidency," apparently published as the article listed at Entry D181.

G189   Meserve, Hamilton W. "Corwin Chides Wilson For 'Stubborn' Policy." Daily Princetonian, April 19, 1956, p. 1.

Reviews Corwin's lecture on Woodrow Wilson's career, announced in the article listed at Entry G188, and highlights Corwin's criticism of the president for refusing to accept the League of Nations with the reservations endorsed by Henry Cabot Lodge.

G190   Sklar, Robert A. "Candidate's Undergraduate Days." Daily Princetonian, October 31, 1956, pp. 1, 3-4, 6.

Describes Adlai Stevenson's years at Princeton University, and includes statements by Corwin. Stevenson took Corwin's "Constitutional Interpretation" course, and the Professor remembered Stevenson as cocky and "miscast." Corwin stated flatly that Stevenson "just didn't do very well," and that he "wasn't quite ready for it."

G191   Jackson, Roderick C. [Letter to the Editor:] "Electoral System Queried." New York Times, January 10, 1957, p. 28.

Responds to Corwin's letter listed at Entry E52 and outlines historical anomalies in the electoral system.

G192   Sawyer, Henry W. 3rd. [Letter to the Editor:] "Invoking the Fifth Amendment." New York Times, August 31, 1957, p. 14.

Responds to Corwin's letter listed at Entry E54 and criticizes Corwin's narrow view of the Self-Incrimination Clause. The writer shows that the clause has been applicable to any governmental proceeding since 1891.

G193   "Troop Precedent Goes Back to 1792." New York Times, September 25, 1957, p. 14.

Describes early uses of federal troops similar to President Eisenhower's use of troops to control domestic violence surrounding desegregation of schools in Little Rock. Corwin underscores the president's statutory authority to use the troops, regardless of the local government's wishes.

G194   McCuaig, Donald D. "Edward S. Corwin: A Classic in His Lifetime, The Constitutional Authority Is Still an Active Scholar at 79." Princeton Alumni Weekly, November 22, 1957, pp. 8-11.

Provides an insightful, informative, and cautious biography of Corwin, albeit uncritically affectionate. McCuaig reviews Corwin's career as a teacher and scholar and uses interviews and early records to provide solid background data.

G195   Reston, James. "The Presidency--II." New York Times, December 3, 1957, p. 23.

Quotes Corwin on the issue of presidential health and President Eisenhower's handling of health problems. Corwin criticizes Eisenhower's detachment from subordinate officers in the administration.

G196   Black, Charles L., Jr. [Letter to the Editor:] "Role of the Supreme Court." New York Times, March 23, 1958, sec. 4, p. 8.

Criticizes Corwin's letter listed at Entry E55 and supports the Warren Court.

G197   "The Court Assailed Again." Richmond Times-Dispatch, April 3, 1958, p. 12.

Quotes from Corwin's letter listed at Entry E55 and endorses his condemnation of the Warren Court.

G198   Newland, Chester A. "Legal Periodicals and
            the United States Supreme Court." Midwest
            Journal of Political Science 3 (February
            1959): 58-74.

Examines the use of legal periodicals in the written
opinions of Supreme Court justices. The study places
Corwin among the ten most-cited authors.

G199   Reston, James. "What Kind of President Do
            You Want?--III," New York Times, May 11, 1960,
            p. 38.

Quotes from Corwin's book listed at Entry A12.4 on
President Eisenhower's "institutional presidency" and
his detachment from cabinet activities.

G200   Garvey, Gerald. "Corwin on the Constitution:
            The Content and Context of Modern American
            Constitutional Theory." Ph.D. dissertation,
            Princeton University, 1962.

Analyzes Corwin's role in the transition of constitutional theory from the laissez-faire doctrines of 1905
to the "constitutional revolution" beginning with the
New Deal.

G201   "Edward Corwin, Law Expert, Dies." New York
            Times, April 30, 1963, p. 35.

Reports on Corwin's death and provides a general
biographical sketch.

G202   "University Notes." Princeton Alumni Weekly,
            May 10, 1963, p. 5.

Announces Corwin's death on April 29 and provides
a brief description of his achievements.

G203   "Milestones." Time, May 10, 1963, p. 96.

Reports briefly on Corwin's death attributed to
cancer.

G204   Mason, Alpheus Thomas. "In Memoriam: Edward
            Samuel Corwin." American Political Science
            Review 57 (September 1963): 789-790.

Provides an affectionate and informative biography of Corwin, reviewing his teaching and personal manner as well as his scholarly accomplishments.

G205   Mason, Alpheus T. "A Memorial to Edward S. Corwin." Princeton Alumni Weekly, October 22, 1963, pp. 11, 16.

Describes Corwin's career at Princeton University and his style as a scholar and professor. Mason provides an affectionate and lively perspective of Corwin.

G206   Americana Annual, pp. 736-737. New York: Americana Corporation, 1964.

Reports briefly on Corwin's death.

G207   Mason, Alpheus T. and Garvey, Gerald. Introduction to American Constitutional History: Essays by Edward S. Corwin, by Edward S. Corwin. New York: Harper & Row, Publishers, 1964.

        Reprint: Gloucester, Mass.: Peter Smith, 1964.

Introduces a collection of articles and describes generally Corwin's career and theories. The essay focuses primarily on Corwin's theories of judicial review. See Entry A21.

G208   Cushman, Robert E. "Edward Samuel Corwin." In American Philosophical Society Year Book, 1963, pp. 130-133. Philadelphia: American Philosophical Society, 1964.

Presents a highly complimentary and detailed obituary of Corwin. Corwin was a member of the American Philosophical Society, receiving its Phillips Prize (see Entries G128-G130) and delivering important lectures to the group (based on articles listed at Entries D137 and D180). See Entry G123.

G209   Buckley, William F., Jr. "Goldwater and the Court." Washington Daily News, September 16, 1964, p. 29.

Lists Corwin among the detractors of the Warren Court. Buckley cites Corwin's reference to the Court's "aggressive tendencies" from his letter listed at Entry E55.

G210   Newton, Robert E. "Edward S. Corwin and American Constitutional Law." Journal of Public Law 14 (1965): 198-212.

Analyzes the diverse theories and contributions of constitutional law that Corwin studied and developed through his long career. The article makes a general overview of Corwin's major writings and their effects on other scholars and government policies.

G211   Guide to the Archives and Manuscript Collections of the American Philosophical Society. Compiled by Whitfield J. Bell, Jr. and Murphy D. Smith. Philadelphia: American Philosophical Society, 1966.

Lists Corwin at page 18 as a speaker in a series of weekly radio broadcasts sponsored by the American Philosophical Society in 1942-1943 "principally on internationalism in sciences."

G212   Leuchtenburg, William E. "The Origins of Franklin D. Roosevelt's 'Court-Packing' Plan." In The Supreme Court Review, 1966, edited by Philip B. Kurland, pp. 347-400. Chicago: University of Chicago Press, 1966.

Outlines the events, personalities, and proposals leading to Roosevelt's adoption of the Court-packing plan. Leuchtenburg includes a substantial examination of Corwin's role as an advisor in the Justice Department. By examining Corwin's correspondence, the essay reveals the Professor's contribution of linking a mandatory retirement age with the desire for fresh Court appointees.

G213   Faulkner, Robert K. "John Marshall and the Burr Trial." Journal of American History 53 (September 1966): 247-258.

Analyzes John Marshall's conduct of the trial of Aaron Burr and criticizes Corwin's conclusion that the trial is "the one serious blemish" on Marshall's judicial record.

G214   Faulkner, Robert Kenneth. "Appendix 2: Mar-
          shall and the Burr Trial." In The Jurispru-
          dence of John Marshall, pp. 269-285. Prince-
          ton: Princeton University Press, 1968.

Revised from the article listed at Entry G213.

G215   Garvey, Gerald. "Scholar in Politics: Edward
          S. Corwin and the 1937 Court-packing Battle."
          Princeton University Library Chronicle 31
          (Autumn 1969): 1-11.

Reviews in detail Corwin's role in the Court-packing
proposal. Garvey uses Corwin's personal correspondence
to give the article depth and character. The author
concludes that Corwin's prestige suffered somewhat from
his support for the unpopular plan.

G216   Loss, Richard. Introduction to Presidential
          Power and the Constitution: Essays by Edward
          S. Corwin, by Edward S. Corwin. Ithaca: Cor-
          nell University Press, 1976.

Introduces a collection of Corwin articles on the
presidency and examines some of his related theories.
Loss views Corwin's writings on the presidency in the
context of studies by other authors. See Entry A22.

G217   Loss, Richard. "Edward S. Corwin: The Con-
          stitution of the Dominant Presidency." Presi-
          dential Studies Quarterly 7 (Winter 1977):
          53-65.

Traces Corwin's theory of the dominant, or "aggrandized," presidency from its inception through the remain-
der of Corwin's writing career. The article analyzes
Corwin's opinions in the context of his general belief
that the Constitution is "living" and must serve modern
needs, regardless of the framers' intentions.

G218   "Corwin, Edward S." In A Princeton Companion,
          edited by Alexander Leitch, pp. 118-120.
          Princeton: Princeton University Press, 1978.

Presents a general brief biography of Corwin. The
book mentions Corwin at several other places throughout.

G219   Garvey, Gerald. "Corwin, Edward S." In International Encyclopedia of the Social Sciences, edited by David L. Sills, vol. 18, pp. 129-132. New York: The Free Press, 1979.

Outlines briefly Corwin's intellectual career from his early writings on fundamental constitutional law, through the New Deal, to his later writings on the presidency. The essay highlights some of Corwin's important writings and theories and demonstrates certain changes in the Professor's thoughts. Garvey gives special attention to the articles listed at Entries D63, D71, and D72.

G220   Mason, Alpheus Thomas. "Corwin, Edward Samuel." In Dictionary of American Biography, supp. 7, pp. 146-147. Edited by John A. Garraty. New York: Charles Scribner's Sons, 1981.

Presents a standard biography of Corwin with some personal insight by Mason, one of Corwin's Princeton colleagues.

G221   Loss, Richard. Introduction to Corwin on the Constitution, by Edward S. Corwin. Vol. 1, The Foundations of American Constitutional and Political Thought, the Powers of Congress, and the President's Power of Removal, edited by Richard Loss, pp. 17-43. Ithaca: Cornell University Press, 1981.

Analyzes Corwin's writings republished in the book listed at Entry A23, giving emphasis to Corwin's theories of "higher law," "natural law," and the president's removal power. See Entry G222.

G222   Loss, Richard. "Corwin on Alexander Hamilton and the President's Removal Power." In Corwin on the Constitution, by Edward S. Corwin. Vol. 1, The Foundations of American Constitutional and Political Thought, the Powers of Congress, and the President's Power of Removal, edited by Richard Loss, pp. 373-377. Ithaca: Cornell University Press, 1981.

Criticizes Corwin's reading of the Federalist Papers, particularly his apparent disregard of Hamilton's views of the president's removal power. See Entries A23, G221, and G225.

G223   Konefsky, Alfred S. "Men of Great and Little
        Faith: Generations of Constitutional Schol-
        ars." Buffalo Law Review 30 (Spring 1981):
        365-384.

Examines the careers and theories of seven constitutional scholars: Corwin, Charles Grove Haines, Alpheus
T. Mason, Carl Swisher, Felix Frankfurter, Alexander
Bickel, and Gerald Gunther. Konefsky finds that Corwin's
principal objective underlying his theories was a desire
to preserve and promote democracy as a means of assuring
freedom. But the author argues that the actual problem
Corwin challenged was capitalism's effects on social
welfare.

G224   Bailey, Harry A., Jr. "Neustadt's Thesis Re-
        visited: Toward the Two Faces of Presidential
        Power." Presidential Studies Quarterly 11
        (Summer 1981): 351-357.

Compares Richard Neustadt's theories of fluid presidential powers to the theories of various other authors,
including Corwin. The analysis emphasizes the rigid
structure of Corwin's institutional presidency model.
The article is from a symposium on Neustadt's theories
[Presidential Studies Quarterly 11 (Summer 1981): 341-
363] which mentions Corwin at several other places.

G225   Loss, Richard. "Alexander Hamilton and the
        Modern Presidency: Continuity or Discontinu-
        ity?" Presidential Studies Quarterly 12 (Win-
        ter 1982): 6-25.

Demonstrates that Corwin's presidential theories do
not adhere to Hamilton's writings in the Federalist
Papers, despite Corwin's statements to the contrary.
Loss also makes a similar analysis of Hamilton's influ-
ence on Theodore Roosevelt and Woodrow Wilson. See Entry
G222.

NOTES
SUBJECT INDEX
PERIODICALS INDEX

Notes

References in the notes to writings by Edward S. Corwin abbreviate the author as "ESC." References to the "ESC Papers" are to the Edward S. Corwin Papers, Seeley G. Mudd Manuscript Library, Princeton University.

Notes to the Preface
Pages xi to xiv

1. Arthur M. Schlesinger, Jr., The Imperial Presidency (Boston: Houghton Mifflin Company, 1973), 139. Louis W. Koenig, review of Corwin on the Constitution, vol. 1, edited by Richard Loss, Presidential Studies Quarterly 12 (Spring 1982): 273.

2. "Writings of Edward S. Corwin," in American Constitutional History: Essays by Edward S. Corwin, ed. Alpheus T. Mason and Gerald Garvey (New York: Harper & Row, Publishers, 1964), 216-219. "Additions to the Mason-Garvey Bibliography," in Presidential Power and the Constitution: Essays by Edward S. Corwin, ed. Richard Loss (Ithaca: Cornell University Press, 1976), 177.

3. ESC, The President: Office and Powers (New York: New York University Press, 1940), vii.

Notes to Chapter One
Pages 3 to 15

1. ESC, "Edward Corwin Requests By-Pass for Princeton," Princeton Herald, August 1, 1951, p. 4.

2. "Information for the National Cyclopaedia of American Biography," n.d. ca. 1946, ESC Papers, Box 3.

3. The Corwin lineage and many of the basic facts about Corwin's birth and education are from "Corwin, Edward Samuel," in National Cyclopaedia of American Biography (New York: James T. White & Company, 1946), Current Vol. G, p. 511.

4. Frances Dwight Buell, "Edward S. Corwin" (unpublished essay, April 1959, courtesy of Mrs. Buell), 1-2.

5. Donald D. McCuaig, "Edward S. Corwin: A Classic in His Lifetime, The Constitutional Authority Is Still an Active Scholar at 79," Princeton Alumni Weekly, November 22, 1957, p. 8. Corwin's undergraduate curriculum is described in Frank E. Robbins to Mrs. R. L. Buell, June 5, 1959 (courtesy of Frances Dwight Buell).

6. Frank E. Robbins to Mrs. R. L. Buell, June 5, 1959 (courtesy of Frances Dwight Buell). ESC to Frances Dwight Buell, July 27, 1959 (courtesy of Frances Dwight Buell).

7. ESC, Liberty Against Government (Baton Rouge: Louisiana State University Press, 1948), xi. Henry Steele Commager, "McLaughlin, Andrew Cunningham," in Dictionary of American Biography, ed. John A. Garraty and Edward T. James (New York: Charles Scribner's Sons, 1974), supp. 4, pp. 530-532.

8. Thomas S. Ganclay to ESC, May 24, 1958, ESC Papers, Box 2. "Who's Who in the Alumni University," Michigan Alumnus, May 6, 1933, p. 474.

9. Principal of The Polytechnic Institute to ESC, September 1, 1901, ESC Papers, Box 2.

10. Alpheus Thomas Mason, "In Memoriam: Edward Samuel Corwin," American Political Science Review 57 (September 1963): 789-790. Corwin's educational credentials are summarized in Wilson's report to the Board of Trustees of Princeton University, December 14, 1905, published in Arthur S. Link, ed., The Papers of Woodrow Wilson (Princeton: Princeton University Press, 1973), 16:250. Corwin's dissertation was published as French Policy and the American Alliance of 1778 (Princeton: Princeton University Press, 1916).

11. ESC, "Departmental Colleague," in Woodrow Wilson: Some Princeton Memories, ed. William Starr Myers (Princeton: Princeton University Press, 1946), 19. John S. Brubacher and Willis Rudy, Higher Education in

Transition: A History of American Colleges and Universities, 1636-1976, 3rd ed. (New York: Harper & Row,
Publishers, 1976), 268.

12. ESC, "Departmental Colleague," 19. Jeremiah
S. Finch, "Preceptorial method," in A Princeton Companion, ed. Alexander Leitch (Princeton: Princeton University Press, 1978), 374.

13. ESC, "Departmental Colleague," 19-20. Alpheus
Thomas Mason, "Politics, The Department of," in A Princeton Companion, ed. Alexander Leitch (Princeton: Princeton University Press, 1978), 370. ESC to Woodrow Wilson, June 3, 1905, and Wilson's report to the Board of
Trustees of Princeton University, June 12, 1905, both
in Link, ed., Papers of Wilson, 16:110, 131.

14. The "short and stocky" description is in Louis
M. Lyons, "The World's Wise Men," Boston Globe, June
19, 1936, p. 20. Leda Boechat Rodrigues, "A life devoted
to American Constitutional Law" (English translation
by Rodriguez of a Portuguese article about Corwin published in Revista Brasileira de Estudos Politicos 3 (July
1959): 23-48), p. 1, Princeton University Archives,
Corwin File. Corwin's speaking style and the "dishulroo"
incident are in McCuaig, "Edward S. Corwin," 10-11.

15. McCuaig, "Edward S. Corwin," 10. ESC to Senator H. Alexander Smith, October 22, 1945, ESC Papers,
Box 1.

16. Charles G. Osgood, Lights in Nassau Hall
(Princeton: Princeton University Press, 1951), 34.
Jeremiah S. Finch, "Preceptorial method," 374.

17. ESC, "The Princeton Preceptorial System," Michigan Alumnus 12 (March 1906): 269-272. ESC, "Departmental Colleague," 22-23. Osgood, Lights, 35.

18. ESC, "Departmental Colleague," 20-21. ESC,
"The Princeton Preceptorial System," 272.

19. ESC, "The Princeton Preceptorial System," 271.
Woodrow Wilson's report to the Board of Trustees of
Princeton University, June 11, 1906, in Link, ed. Papers
of Wilson, 16:421.

20. For a general description of the "quad plan"
controversy, see Arthur S. Link, Wilson: The Road to
the White House (Princeton: Princeton University Press,
1947), 45-57. ESC, "Departmental Colleague," 28-29.
Minutes of a meeting of the Princeton faculty, September
30, 1907, in Link, ed., Papers of Wilson, 17:407-408.

21. Buell, "Edward S. Corwin," 9. For a general analysis of the relationship between Wilson and Roosevelt, including references to Corwin's opinions, see John Milton Cooper, Jr., The Warrior and the Priest: Woodrow Wilson and Theodore Roosevelt (Cambridge: The Belknap Press of Harvard University Press, 1983).

22. ESC, "Departmental Colleague," 27. "From the Diary of William Starr Myers," May 8, 1908, in Link, ed., Papers of Wilson, 18:293-294.

23. ESC, "Departmental Colleague," 24. McCuaig, "Edward S. Corwin," 9. Wilson had previously and unsuccessfully passed Corwin's name to Houghton, Mifflin and Company as a possible author for an American history textbook. Woodrow Wilson to Houghton, Mifflin and Company, May 26, 1908, in Link, ed., Papers of Wilson, 20:483.

24. ESC, "Departmental Colleague," 24-25. McCuaig, "Edward S. Corwin," 9. "Corwin, Edward Samuel," in National Cyclopaedia of American Biography.

25. Dedication to ESC, The President: Office and Powers (New York: New York University Press, 1940).

26. An insightful and complimentary review of Corwin's early articles appears in "Edward S. Corwin: Critic of American Constitutional Theory," Green Bag 26 (October 1914): 435-439. Woodrow Wilson to Winthrop More Daniels, May 10, 1910, in Link, ed., Papers of Wilson, 20:430.

27. For a general history of Wilson's departure from Princeton and his election to the presidency, see Link, Road to the White House.

28. ESC, "Departmental Colleague," 29. Link, Road to the White House, 442-445.

29. ESC, "Departmental Colleague," 30-31. ESC to Woodrow Wilson, April 13, 1913, and Woodrow Wilson to ESC, April 19, 1913, in Link, ed., Papers of Wilson, 27:299, 336.

30. ESC, National Supremacy: Treaty Power vs. State Power (New York: Henry Holt and Company, 1913). ESC, "Departmental Colleague," 31. ESC to Theodore Roosevelt, September 30, 1913, and Theodore Roosevelt to ESC, October 3, 1913, Theodore Roosevelt Papers, Library of Congress.

31. ESC, "A 'Firm' Foreign Policy," New York Evening Post, October 26, 1916, p. 8. Years later, Corwin reflected, "I had voted for Mr. Wilson in 1912 with great enthusiasm and for Mr. Hughes in 1916 with somewhat less enthusiasm." ESC, "Departmental Colleague," 25.

32. ESC, "Pacifism Constitutes New National Problem," Daily Princetonian, March 27, 1917, pp. 1, 4.

33. ESC, "Conscription Only Is Efficient and Reliable," Daily Princetonian, April 14, 1917, pp. 1, 4. ESC, "Concerning Mr. Angell," Daily Princetonian, February 26, 1916, p. 2.

34. U.S. Committee on Public Information, War Cyclopedia: A Handbook for Ready Reference on the Great War, (Washington: Government Printing Office, 1918). "R.O.T.C. Announcement," Daily Princetonian, March 5, 1918, p. 1. Princeton in the World War (Princeton: Princeton University Press, 1932), 590.

35. E. C. Otte, Norway, Sweden and Denmark, vol. 16 of The History of Nations (Philadelphia: J. D. Morris and Company, 1907).

36. ESC, "The Freedom of the Seas," North American Review 209 (January 1919): 29-42. "The Freedom of the Seas," The American Review of Reviews 59 (February 1919): 196-197. ESC, "Freedom of the Seas Discussed by Corwin," Daily Princetonian, February 18, 1919, pp. 1, 4. ESC, "Freedom of the Seas--A Compromise," Nation, March 8, 1919, pp. 365-367.

37. ESC, "An Examination of the Covenant," Review, June 7, 1919, pp. 77-80. "Wilson's Friend Flays League at Hoboken Forum," Hudson Observer, clipping in ESC Papers, Box 18, marked "Sept. or Oct. 7, 1919."

Notes to Chapter Two
Pages 17 to 22

1. "Edward S. Corwin: Critic of American Constitutional Theory," Green Bag 26 (October 1914): 435-439. ESC, "Some Possibilities in the Way of Treaty-Making," in Report of the Twentieth Annual Lake Mohonk Conference on International Arbitration, ed. H. C. Phillips (Lake Mohonk, N. Y.: Lake Mohonk Conference on International Arbitration, 1914), 65-70.

2. ESC, "The Worship of the Constitution," Constitutional Review 4 (January 1920): 3-11.

3. ESC, "The Spending Power of Congress--Apropos the Maternity Act," Harvard Law Review 36 (March 1923): 548-582. ESC, "Game Protection and the Constitution," Michigan Law Review 14 (June 1916): 613-625.

4. ESC, "An Examination of the Covenant," Review, June 7, 1919, pp. 77-80. ESC, "The Permanent Court of International Justice," Weekly Review, September 29, 1920, p. 265. ESC, "Corwin, Gauss, and Van Dyke Give Views on Court, Advising American Adherence," Daily Princetonian (World Court Supplement), November 25, 1925, pp. 3-4. ESC, "The League and the Court," New York Times, September 29, 1920, p. 8. "The Week," Harvey's Weekly, October 23, 1920, p. 3.

5. Frances Dwight Buell, "Edward S. Corwin" (unpublished essay, April 1959, courtesy of Mrs. Buell), 1. Professor Walter Francis Murphy to author, n.d. November 1976.

6. Harold Gill Reuschlein, Jurisprudence--Its American Prophets: A Survey of Taught Jurisprudence (Indianapolis: The Bobbs-Merrill Company, Inc., 1951), 342-345. ESC, The Constitution and What It Means Today (Princeton: Princeton University Press, 1920).

7. Benjamin N. Cardozo to ESC, July 31, 1925, ESC Papers, Box 1. ESC, John Marshall and the Constitution: A Chronicle of the Supreme Court, vol. 16 of The Chronicles of America Series (New Haven: Yale University Press, 1919). McCulloch v. Maryland, 17 U.S. (4 Wheat.) 316, 415 (1819) (emphasis in original).

8. Paul L. Haworth to ESC, February 8, 1936, ESC Papers, Box 2. ESC to Dana Ferrin, January 10, 1938, ESC Papers, Box 3. American Philosophical Society Year Book, 1938 (Philadelphia: American Philosophical Society, 1939), 45.

9. "Princeton Teachers Stand with Scopes," New York Times, July 18, 1925, p. 2. "Defeat of Drys on Beer Test in High Court Predicted by Prof. Corwin of Princeton," New York Times, March 20, 1933, p. 3. "How To Reduce Crime," Atlanta Journal, July 17, 1927, p. 15. ESC, "Freedom of Speech and the Press Under the First Amendment: A Resume," Yale Law Journal 30 (November 1920): 48-55.

10. Alpheus Thomas Mason, "Politics, The Department of," in A Princeton Companion, ed. Alexander Leitch (Princeton: Princeton University Press, 1978), 370, 372. Alpheus T. Mason, "A Memorial to Edward S. Corwin," Princeton Alumni Weekly, October 22, 1963, p. 11. Donald

D. McCuaig, "Edward S. Corwin: A Classic in His Lifetime, The Constitutional Authority Is Still an Active
Scholar at 79," Princeton Alumni Weekly, November 22,
1957, pp. 8-11.

11.   McCuaig, "Edward S. Corwin," 8.   "Corwin,
Edward S.," in International Encyclopedia of the Social
Sciences, ed. David L. Sills (New York: The Free Press,
1978): 18:129-132.   "Corwin Upholds Lectures as Being
Useful Method," Daily Princetonian, February 2, 1926,
pp. 1, 4.   ESC, "Rebukes Communication of '1928'," Daily
Princetonian, December 12, 1927, p. 2.   The following
three citations refer to well-known persons who studied
under Corwin.   Mason, "Politics," 370.   Buell, "Edward
S. Corwin," 7.   Robert A. Sklar, "Candidate's Undergraduate Days," Daily Princetonian, October 31, 1956,
pp. 1, 3-4, 6.   The reference to co-educational teaching
is from W. A. Bours III and J. S. Shirk, "'Sunflower
has Gone to Seed,' Claims Corwin, Who Sees Roosevelt
as Having Done 'Good Job'," Daily Princetonian, October
29, 1936, pp. 1, 6.

12.   McCuaig, "Edward S. Corwin," 10.   Buell, "Edward S. Corwin," 2.

13.   McCuaig, "Edward S. Corwin," 9.   "Federal System Held China's Needs," New York Times, May 5, 1929,
sec. 2, p. 4.   "China's Problems Called One of Economics," New York World, June 2, 1929, sec. 6, p. 12.
"Prof. Corwin Says Orient is Restless," Daily Princetonian, April 23, 1929, pp. 1, 3.   ESC, "Yenching University: A Unique Institution in China" (unpublished essay,
April 23, 1929, ESC Papers, Box 27), 1-2.

14.   McCuaig, "Edward S. Corwin," 9.   "China's Problems Called One of Economics," New York World, June 2,
1929, sec. 6, p. 12.   Passenger lists from ships on which
the Corwins sailed during their China venture are in
the ESC Papers, Box 27:   the "List of Passengers" from
the S. S. Rawalpindi shows that they left Bombay for
Marseilles on March 16, 1929; the "Guest List" from the
S. S. Ruth Alexander shows that they left Marseilles
for the United States on April 3, 1929.   "Students Gather
for International Relations Parley," Durham Morning Herald, February 27, 1931, pp. 1, 9.

15.   "Seventeen Little Deans," Princeton Alumni
Weekly, June 9, 1933, p. 774.

Notes to Chapter Three
Pages 23 to 32

1. W. A. Bours III and J. S. Shirk, "'Sunflower Has Gone to Seed,' Claims Corwin, Who Sees Roosevelt as Having Done 'Good Job'," Daily Princetonian, October 29, 1936, pp. 1, 6. For a general survey of Franklin Roosevelt and the New Deal, see James MacGregor Burns, Roosevelt: The Lion and the Fox (New York: Harcourt, Brace & World, Inc., 1956).

2. "NRA Constitutional, Prof. Corwin Says," New York Times, November 7, 1933, p. 3.

3. ESC, "The Establishment of Judicial Review" [part 2], Michigan Law Review 9 (February 1911): 316. ESC, "Marbury v. Madison and the Doctrine of Judicial Review," Michigan Law Review 12 (May 1914): 572 (emphasis in original). ESC, review of Social Reform and the Constitution, by Frank J. Goodnow, American Political Science Review 6 (May 1912): 276. ESC, "President, Court and Constitution" [part 2], Christian Science Monitor, July 5, 1935, p. 18.

4. "NRA Constitutional, Prof. Corwin Says," New York Times, November 7, 1933, p. 3. ESC, The Twilight of the Supreme Court (New Haven: Yale University Press, 1934), 148. ESC, "Some Probable Repercussions of 'Nira' on Our Constitutional System," Annals of the American Academy of Political and Social Science 172 (March 1934): 143-144.

5. ESC, The President: Office and Powers (New York: New York University Press, 1948), 236. ESC, "Wilson and the Senate," Review, July 26, 1919, pp. 228-229. ESC, "The Power of the Supreme Court Over Legislation," New York Law Journal, January 21, 1925, p. 1506. ESC, "The Power of the Supreme Court Over Legislation," Chicago Legal News, February 5, 1925, p. 231. "Beveridge Upholds Powers of Courts," New York Times, January 21, 1925, p. 2.

6. ESC, "Constitutional Questions in the New Legislation: Outline and Summary of Remarks by Edward S. Corwin," Princeton University Alumni Lectures, June 15 and 16, 1933, pp. 17-18.

7. Home Building & Loan Association v. Blaisdell, 290 U.S. 398 (1934). "Professor Corwin on Minnesota Case," New York Times, January 11, 1934, p. 16.

8. "Job-Insurance Plan Fought by Labor Leaders," New York Herald Tribune, February 18, 1935, p. 30. For

criticism of Corwin's New Deal analyses, see Richard Loss, "Edward S. Corwin: The Constitution of the Dominant Presidency," Presidential Studies Quarterly 7 (Winter 1977): 58. A. R. Clas, Director of Housing, to ESC, June 15, 1935, ESC Papers, Box 2. The Justice Department also employed Corwin as an "expert witness" on the case of Pulaski v. Newark Milk Company. S. A. Andretta to Robert H. Jackson, October 16, 1936, ESC Papers, Box 1. Thurman Arnold explained to Corwin that the "expert witness" title was appropriate, because Corwin was giving the government information rather than acting as counsel on record. Thurman Arnold to ESC, October 21, 1936, ESC Papers, Box 1.

9. Benjamin Cardozo to ESC, November 16, 1935, ESC Papers, Box 1. Thurman Arnold to ESC, October 5, 1936, ESC Papers, Box 1.

10. Carter v. Carter Coal Co., 298 U.S. 238 (1936). David Lawrence, "Guffey Act Issue Considered Reargument of Imperfectly Settled NRA Questions," New York Sun, March 13, 1936, p. 17. Lemuel F. Parton, "Dr. Corwin of Princeton Was a Confrere of Woodrow Wilson," New York Sun, March 16, 1936, p. 29. "Judiciary," Time, March 23, 1936, p. 23. Corwin wrote much of the government's brief for the Carter Coal case. Peter H. Irons, The New Deal Lawyers (Princeton: Princeton University Press, 1982), 251.

11. For a general study of the Supreme Court problem during the New Deal, see Burns, Roosevelt. The Court struck down New Deal legislation in the following cases: United States V. Butler, 297 U.S. 1 (1936) (Agricultural Adjustment Act); A.L.A. Schecter Poultry Corp. v. United States, 295 U.S. 1 (1936) (National Industrial Recovery Act); Panama Refining Co. v. Ryan, 293 U.S. 388 (1935) (NIRA); Carter v. Carter Coal Co., 298 U.S. 238 (1936) (Bituminous Coal Conservation Act).

12. Corwin wrote a series of three articles for the Christian Science Monitor and a series of five for the Philadelphia Record. The second set also appeared in the Washington Post, the New York Evening Post, and the Progressive. His radio lecture is published as ESC, "Curbing the Court," Annals of the American Academy of Political and Social Science 185 (May 1936): 45-55. Corwin's comments to his students appear in Gerald Garvey, "Scholar in Politics: Edward S. Corwin and the 1937 Court-packing Battle," Princeton University Library Chronicle 31 (Autumn 1969): 7. Louis M. Lyons, "The World's Wise Men," Boston Globe, June 19, 1936, p. 20. Douglas Campbell to ESC, February 8, 1937, ESC Papers, Box 2.

13. Bours and Shirk, "Sunflower," Daily Princeton-ian, October 29, 1936, pp. 1, 6. "How They Are Voting," New Republic, September 30, 1936, pp. 223-224.

14. Corwin's speech at Harvard is published at ESC, "The Constitution as Instrument and as Symbol," American Political Science Review 30 (December 1936): 1071-1085. The original article about the Supreme Court doors is "'Error' Found in Supreme Court, But It's in the Art of a Door Panel," New York Times, July 5, 1936, sec. 2, p. 1. The Washington Evening Star and Washington Daily News reported the controversy Corwin stirred during September 1936. Corwin's letter of response is ESC to Cass Gilbert, Jr., October 14, 1936, ESC Papers, Box 2. The Hughes quotation controversy is reported at Tully Nettleton, "Tracking a Quotation to Its Lair," Christian Science Monitor, March 9, 1935, p. 16.

15. ESC, "Reform by Amendment Slow and Undemocrat-ic," Philadelphia Record, November 30, 1936, pp. 1-2. ESC, "Theory of 'Finality' Of Rulings Collapses," Phila-delphia Record, December 2, 1936, sec. 1, p. 12. ESC, "Court Should Make Only Unanimous Veto," Philadelphia Record, December 4, 1936, sec. 1, p. 19. William E. Leuchtenburg, "The Origins of Franklin D. Roosevelt's 'Court-Packing' Plan," in The Supreme Court Review, 1966, ed. Philip B. Kurland (Chicago: University of Chicago Press, 1966): 387-390.

16. ESC, "Judicial Review in Action," University of Pennsylvania Law Review 74 (May 1926): 653. ESC, "Congress, Supreme Court Could Solve Constitutional 'New Deal' Issues," Progressive, January 16, 1937, p. 7.

17. U.S. Congress, Senate Committee on the Judi-ciary, Reorganization of the Federal Judiciary: Hearings before the Committee on the Judiciary on S. 1392, part 2, 75th Cong., 1st sess., 1937, 167-225. "Savant In-dorses F.D.R. Court Plan," Atlanta Constitution, February 8, 1937, pp. 1, 3. "Question of Dictators," Raleigh News and Observer, February 9, 1937, p. 4. "Corwin Favors Court Reform," New York Times, February 9, 1937, p. 4.

18. ESC to Arthur N. Holcombe, December 9, 1936, ESC Papers, Box 1. Leuchtenburg, "Origins," 390. Abe Glasser to ESC, February 8, 1937, ESC Papers, Box 2. At least one historian has flatly concluded that Roose-velt "consulted" Corwin, but that statement is not sup-portable. Michael E. Parrish, Felix Frankfurter and His Times: The Reform Years (New York: The Free Press, 1982), 267.

19. U.S. Congress, Reorganization of the Federal Judiciary, 167-225. G. Gould Lincoln, "Educator Views 'Economic Bias' Swaying Court," Washington Evening Star, March 17, 1937, sec. A, pp. 1, 5. "Corwin Assails Court View of Constitution," New York Sun, March 17, 1937, p. 16. "Most Justices Wrong on Constitution, Professor Tells Senate's Hearing," New York World-Telegram, March 17, 1937, p. 2. Turner Catledge, "Justices Pressed for Court Views," New York Times, March 18, 1937, p. 18. Robert C. Albright, "Corwin Urges 15-Judge Court With Three Functioning Panels," Washington Post, March 18, 1937, pp. 1, 5. "9 Justices Urged To State Views on Court Curb Plan," New York Herald Tribune, March 18, 1937, pp. 1, 13.

20. U.S. Congress, Reorganization of the Federal Judiciary, 167-225.

21. The hearing transcript did not capture Corwin's self-evaluative "I live and learn," although the press reported the remark. "Live and Learn," New York Times, March 19, 1937, p. 22. "Corwin vs. Consistency," Daily Princetonian, March 20, 1937, p. 2. "Academic Freedom in Discussing the Supreme Court," Princeton Alumni Weekly, April 2, 1937, p. 550. John Bennett to ESC, March 17, 1937, ESC Papers, Box 2.

22. The Dodds and McLaughlin comments are in "The Question of the Week: Should Congress Approve or Disapprove Plan to Increase Size of Supreme Court?" United States News, February 15, 1937, p. 4. The Brookings Institution report is published as Memorandum of the Special Committee on the Constitution: Special Committee Memoranda Number One (Washington, D.C.: The National Policy Committee, 1937).

23. NLRB v. Jones & Laughlin Steel Corp., 301 U.S. 1 (1937).

24. U.S. Congress, Reorganization of the Federal Judiciary, 167-225. W. A. Bours III, "New Roosevelt Bill to Remodel Courts Approved by Corwin," Daily Princetonian, February 12, 1937, p. 1. ESC, "The Supreme Court: Prophecy," Campus: America's College and University Newsfeature Magazine, ca. February-April 1937, pp. 48-49 (a copy of the article is the ESC Papers, Box 13; the periodical apparently was a national supplement for college newspapers and is not catalogued at any library).

25. ESC, "Statesmanship on the Supreme Court," American Scholar 9 (Spring 1940): 162. ESC, "The Court Sees a New Light," New Republic, August 4, 1937, pp. 354-

204 / Edward S. Corwin

357. Norman Howden, "CIO Bearing in Court Ruling Cited," Rochester Democrat and Chronicle, April 15, 1937, p. 21.

26. Frances Dwight Buell, "Edward S. Corwin" (unpublished essay, April 1959, courtesy of Mrs. Buell), 10.

Notes to Chapter Four
Pages 33 to 40

1. ESC, "U.S. Begins an Experiment: Will the Neutrality Act Work?" Newsweek, November 6, 1939, pp. 24-25. ESC, The President: Office and Powers (New York: New York University Press, 1940), 135.

2. ESC, Total War and the Constitution (New York: Alfred A. Knopf, 1947), 33, 37, 154.

3. ESC, "The League, the Constitution, and Governor Cox," Weekly Review, August 25, 1920, p. 166. ESC, "Convoys Debated," New York Times, February 23, 1941, sec. 4, p. 9. ESC, "The President's Power," New Republic, January 29, 1951, p. 15.

4. ESC, The President.

5. In the first edition, Corwin simply acknowledged the president's authority to make executive agreements. ESC, The President, 261. ESC, "Executive Authority Held Exceeded in Destroyer Deal," New York Times, October 13, 1940, sec. 4, p. 7. ESC, Total War, 159.

6. ESC, The Constitution and World Organization (Princeton: Princeton University Press, 1944), 40-41.

7. ESC, "Constitutional Aspects of Federal Housing," University of Pennsylvania Law Review 84 (December 1935): 156. ESC, "The War and the Constitution: President and Congress," American Political Science Review 37 (February 1943): 20. ESC, "The President as Administrative Chief," Journal of Politics 1 (February 1939): 43.

8. ESC, The President's Control of Foreign Relations (Princeton: Princeton University Press, 1917), 5. ESC, "The Presidency," Princeton Alumni Weekly, October 22, 1924, p. 80.

9. "How To Reduce Crime," Atlanta Journal, July 27, 1927, p. 15. W. A. Bours III and J. S. Shirk, "'Sunflower Has Gone to Seed,' Claims Corwin, Who Sees Roosevelt as Having Done 'Good Job'," Daily Princetonian,

October 29, 1936, pp. 1, 6. ESC, "E. S. Corwin Comes Out in Support of Willkie Because of Third Term and Foreign Relations," Daily Princetonian, October 26, 1940, pp. 1, 3 (emphasis in original).

10. ESC, "Corwin Comes Out in Support of Willkie," Daily Princetonian, 1. Fred Hogue, "Constitution Amending Declared Outmoded," Los Angeles Times, January 30, 1941, p. 11.

11. ESC, "Corwin Comes Out in Support of Willkie," Daily Princetonian, 3. ESC, The President, 303-306. Raymond L. Buell to ESC, October 13, 1940, ESC Papers, Box 1.

12. ESC, "The War and the Constitution," 19.

13. ESC, The President, 3rd ed., 303-304, 306-307. ESC, "The War and the Constitution," 25. ESC, Total War, 158, 160, 180-181. ESC, review of The Growth of American Constitutional Law, by Benjamin F. Wright, Harvard Law Review 56 (November 1942): 487.

14. ESC, The President, 95, 125. ESC, The President, 3rd ed., 158, 160. ESC, "The Question of the Week: Would Ending of President's Lend-Lease Power By Congressional Resolution Be Constitutional?" United States News, February 28, 1941, pp. 28-29. The Supreme Court ruled in 1983 that legislative vetoes are unconstitutional. INS v. Chadha, 51 U.S.L.W. 4907 (1983).

15. ESC, "Our Expendable Constitution," University of Illinois Bulletin 52 (January 1955): 8. ESC and Louis W. Koenig, The Presidency Today (New York: New York University Press, 1956), 63. Lawrence E. Davies, "Congress Leaders Urged in Cabinet," New York Times, November 23, 1940, p. 19. ESC, The President, 281, 306. ESC, The President, 3rd ed., 363.

16. Frances B. Labue, "Prof. Corwin Believes John L. Lewis' Tactics Will Prove Detrimental to Labor in Long Run," Baton Rouge State-Times, May 7, 1943, p. 6. ESC, "Decline of the Executive," New Republic, June 15, 1953, p. 2.

17. "Goodbye Now," Time, July 15, 1946, p. 70.

Notes to Chapter Five
Pages 41 to 48

1. Department of the Air Force, Notification of Personnel Action, April 23, 1948, ESC Papers, Box 3. U.S. Congress, Senate, The Constitution of the United States of America: Analysis and Interpretation, S. Doc. 170, 82nd Cong., 2nd sess., 1953.

2. ESC, "The Supreme Court as National School Board," Thought 23 (December 1948): 665-683. ESC, "The Supreme Court as National School Board," Law and Contemporary Problems 14 (Winter 1949): 3-22. "Decision on Study of Religion Scored," New York Times, October 15, 1948, p. 20. "Corwin Attacks Ruling In Champaign Case," Christian Century, October 27, 1948, p. 1133. "Corwin scores McCollum decision," America, October 30, 1948, pp. 90-91.

3. ESC to Father Robert Hartnett, S.J., February 8, 1950, ESC Papers, Box 1.

4. ESC, "Vatican Post Discussed," New York Times, November 12, 1951, p. 24. "Dr. Corwin on Vatican envoy," America, November 24, 1951, p. 197. "Princeton Law Professor Defends Vatican Envoy," Catholic News, November 17, 1951, p. 9. ESC, "The Mark Clark Appointment," Catholic Digest 16 (January 1952): 86-88. ESC, "Representation at the Vatican," Catholic Mind 50 (February 1952): 76-78.

5. Corwin espoused narrow civil liberty theories regarding free speech and rights of the accused. ESC, "Freedom of Speech and the Press Under the First Amendment," Yale Law Journal 30 (November 1920): 48-55. "How To Reduce Crime," Atlanta Journal, July 17, 1927, p. 15.

6. Brown v. Board of Education, 347 U.S. 483 (1954). "Professor, Students Take Part In Panel Segregation Conference," Daily Princetonian, November 11, 1954, pp. 2-4. Peter Kihss, "Experts Approve Timetable on Bias," New York Times, May 18, 1954, p. 18.

7. Frances Dwight Buell, "Edward S. Corwin," (unpublished essay, April 1959, courtesy of Mrs. Buell), 12. ESC to Dr. William S. Dix, June 26, 1957, ESC Papers, Box 2.

8. Bruce Bliven, "27 Who Believed in Justice," New Republic, October 22, 1951, pp. 13-15. NAACP Annual Report, 1951 (New York: National Association for the Advancement of Colored People, 1952), 59-60. NAACP

Annual Report, 1952 (New York: National Association for the Advancement of Colored People, 1953), 66.

9. "Leaders to Fight Bricker Proposal," New York Times, December 28, 1953, p. 3. "Group Here Fights Bricker Proposal," New York Times, February 4, 1954, p. 14. Corwin delineated his position on the Bricker Amendment in ESC, "Case Against Bricker Amendment," New York Herald Tribune, May 23, 1955, p. 14. One conservative newspaper criticized Corwin's opposition in light of his attacks on expanding presidential authority. "The Interventionists Hit the Warpath," Chicago Daily Tribune, January 4, 1954, p. 22.

10. Donald D. McCuaig, "Edward S. Corwin: A Classic in His Lifetime, The Constitutional Authority Is Still an Active Scholar at 79," Princeton Alumni Weekly, November 22, 1957, 10. Buell, "Edward S. Corwin," 11.

11. Buell, "Edward S. Corwin," 11.

12. ESC, "Decline of the Executive," New Republic, June 15, 1953, p. 2.

13. ESC, "Of Presidential Prerogative," Whittier College Bulletin 47 (September 1954): 26.

14. Richard Nixon to ESC, December 23, 1955, ESC Papers, Box 4. Richard Nixon to ESC, April 22, 1959, ESC Papers, Box 4.

15. U.S. Congress, House Committee on the Judiciary, Presidential Inability, 84th Cong., 2nd sess., January 31, 1956, 16-17 ("Reply of Edward S. Corwin, Princeton, N.J."). Eberhard Faber, "Corwin Asks New Law For Presidential Crises," Daily Princetonian, October 13, 1955, pp. 1, 3. ESC, "Presidential Disability," New York Times, April 7, 1957, sec. 4, p. 10. ESC, "Problem of Presidential Disability," New York Herald Tribune, December 4, 1957, p. 24.

16. Buell, "Edward S. Corwin," 13. Corwin wrote to Senator John Kennedy in 1955 asking to be excused from a Senate hearing: "I am just recovering from a painful attack of parotitis . . . and my doctor strongly advises me against leaving home this winter weather." U.S. Congress, Senate Committee on Government Operations, Hearings to Create Position of Administrative Vice President, 84th Cong., 2nd sess., 1956, 34.

17. "4 to Run Holmes Fund," New York Times, January 10, 1956, p. 15. Luther A. Huston, "History of Court

to Honor Holmes," New York Times, April 15, 1956, p. 80.
The series of books sponsored by the Permanent Committee
for the Oliver Wendell Holmes Devise is History of the
Supreme Court of the United States (New York: Macmillan
Publishing Co., Inc.). Robert Cushman to ESC, April
18, 1957, ESC Papers, Box 1. Clinton Rossiter to ESC,
July 9, 1957, ESC Papers, Box 1.

18. Buell, "Edward S. Corwin," 13. McCuaig, "Ed-
ward S. Corwin," 10. ESC, "Limiting the Judiciary,"
New York Times, March 16, 1958, sec. 4, p. 10. Although
Corwin was generally critical of the Warren Court, he
did extend a succinct compliment to Justice Harlan:
"Just a line to congratulate you on your opinion in the
NAACP case." The case was NAACP v. Alabama, 357 U.S. 449
(1958). ESC to John Marshall Harlan, July 2, 1958,
Harlan Papers, Princeton University, Box 511.

19. Harold W. Dodds to Dan D. Coyle, April 2, 1963,
Princeton University Archives, Corwin File. "Edward S.
Corwin, Law Expert, Dies," New York Times, April 30,
1963, p. 35.

20. "Corwin Hall," in A Princeton Companion,
ed. Alexander Leitch (Princeton: Princeton University
Press, 1978), 120-121. Alpheus Thomas Mason, "Politics,
The Department of," in A Princeton Companion, 372.

Subject Index

References are to page numbers in the biography and to entry numbers in the bibliography.

Periodicals Index

References are to periodicals listed in all parts of the bibliography.

America, D185, E43, F149, F150, G46, G147, G158

American Bar Association Journal, D131, F59, F110, F120

American Historical Review, D11, D19, D62, D173, E14, E50, F6, F24-F25, F27, F41, F44, F48, F53, F65, F71, F95, F99, F121, F124, F132, F136, G1, G3, G177

American Journal of International Law, F56

American Labor Legislation Review, D100

American Law School Review, D124, G100-G101

American Political Science Review, D41, D43-D45, D47, D57-D58, D63-D64, D73, D77, D102, D138, F5, F8-F10, F12, F14-F15, F17, F21, F23, F26, F32, F34, F42-F43, F60-F62, F67, F70, F72, F75, F77, F82, F85, F87, F97-F98, F101, F107, F111, F127, F133, F137, F140, F148, G21, G111, G204

American Review of Reviews, G9. See also Review of Reviews

American Scholar, D133

Annals of the American Academy of Political and Social Science, D87, D99, D137, F1, F4, F92, F106, F115-F116, F125-F126

Aryan Path, F144

Atlanta Constitution, G84, G133

Atlanta Journal, G28

Baton Rouge State-Times, G131

Boston Globe, G68

Boston University Law Review, D125

Brooklyn Law Review, F102

Buffalo Law Review, G223

Campus, D122

Canadian Historical Review, F122

Catholic Digest, D160, D182

Catholic Mind, D161

Catholic News, G156

Chicago Daily Tribune, G168

About the Author

KENNETH D. CREWS currently practices law in Los Angeles and is a doctoral student at UCLA. His publications appear in history and law journals, and he serves on the History of the Law Committee of the State Bar of California.

Recent Titles in
Bibliographies and Indexes in Law and Political Science

Scottish Nationalism and Cultural Identity in the Twentieth Century: An
Annotated Bibliography of Secondary Sources
Compiled by Gordon Bryan

L368706

Southern Methodist Univ.   fond
KF 4546.A1C74 1985
Edward S. Corwin and the American Consti

3   2177   00234   6938

DATE DUE

GAYLORD			PRINTED IN U.S.A